Pomegranates & Pine Nuts

Pomegranates & Pine Nuts

A stunning collection of Lebanese, Moroccan & Persian recipes

BETHANY KEHDY

DUNCAN BAIRD PUBLISHERS

LONDON

This book is dedicated to my late grandparents, Kehdy Farhoud Kehdy and Adla Kehdy

Pomegranates & Pine Nuts
Bethany Kehdy

Distributed in the USA and Canada by
Sterling Publishing Co., Inc.
387 Park Avenue South,
New York, NY 10016-8810

First published in the UK and USA in 2013 by
Duncan Baird Publishers, an imprint of
Watkins Publishing Limited
Sixth Floor, 75 Wells Street
London W1T 3QH

A member of Osprey Group

Managing Editor: Grace Cheetham
Editor: Alison Bolus
Americanizer: Beverly LeBlanc
Managing Designer: Manisha Patel
Picture Researcher: Emma Copestake
Production: Uzma Taj
Commissioned photography: Šárka Babická
Food Stylist: Emily Jonzen
Prop Stylist: Lucy Harvey

Typeset in Steinem and Andover
Color reproduction by PDQ, UK
Printed in China
ISBN: 978-1-84899-088-3
10 9 8 7 6 5 4 3 2 1

Publisher's note: While every care has been taken in compiling the recipes for this book, Watkins Publishing Limited, or any other persons who have been involved in working on this publication, cannot accept responsibility for any errors or omissions, inadvertent or not, that may be found in the recipes or text, nor for any problems that may arise as a result of preparing one of these recipes. If you are pregnant or breastfeeding or have any special dietary requirements or medical conditions, it is advisable to consult a medical professional before following any of the recipes contained in this book.

Notes on the Recipes
Unless otherwise stated:
Use large eggs and medium fruit and vegetables
Use fresh ingredients, including herbs and chilies
Do not mix metric and imperial measurements
1 tsp. = 5ml   1 tbsp. = 15ml   1 cup = 240ml

For information about custom editions, special sales, premium and corporate purchases, please contact Sterling Special Sales Department at 800-805-5489 or specialsales@sterlingpub.com.

Note on Latinization
Representing Arabic in Latin characters is not a straightforward process at all. As this book covers the expanse of the Middle East and North Africa, I have presupposed an MSA (Modern Standard Arabic) pronunciation for all words transliterated throughout rather than adopting the vernacular or colloquial dialect of my country, Lebanon, which is how I would pronounce the words day to day. That said, in some instances, a regional variation favouring the vernacular pronunciation notable to Lebanon, may still be present. I have tried my best to be as consistent and faithful as possible to the Arabic phonetics and to the best of my knowledge while trying to maintain a balance and accessibility for the non-native speaker so not to alienate them.

Pattern Photo Credits
Murat Cokoker/Shutterstock: 4-5, 14-15, 28-29, 50-51, 56-57, 70-71, 80-81, 88-89, 94-95, 100-101, 116-117, 124-125, 132-133, 140-141, 146-147, 154-155, 160-161, 168-169, 172-173, 180-181, 188-189, 196-197, 204-205, 208, 210, 222.
Eray KULA/Shutterstock: 22-33, 40-41, 66-67.
Javarman/Shutterstock: 98-99, 114-115.

Culinary reflections

beirut, circa 1985. My delicate, fidgeting fingers in the bone-breaking grip of my grandfather's (*jeddo's*) hand, his other hand firmly clasps the daunting, gold, lion-faced ornament mounted on his signature walking stick. As the foot of the stick beats against the asphalt, the thumping sounds are in sync with our steps. Together, we pace down a war-ravaged street in Fassouh, Ashrafieh, en route to my kindergarten. Along the way, we pause by the corner store, where we are greeted by the ruddy-cheeked owner, Rizkallah. Here, my jeddo spoils me with the sweets my young self adored so much. Most notable among them were Tutti Frutti and one we knew as Ras El Abed, with its fez-shaped crunchy outer fortification concealing a soft, meringue interior. As Rizkallah puts them on the counter, my jeddo gestures for me to choose from any one of the sugar-loaded pyramids populating the chilled cabinet. "*Jus ananas, jeddo*," I proclaim—"pineapple juice, grandfather." He then pierces the inconspicuous aluminum-masked porta with the straw, before passing it to me.

The sweets are reserved for *récré*, but only if I am a well-mannered girl, who has eaten all her tartine for lunch. This could be Arabic bread spread with *labneh* (strained yogurt) and dotted with olives, or perhaps cheese and cucumber, ham and cheese or cheese and jam, my grandmother's (*teta's*) favorite. Returning home with the sandwich uneaten isn't something I even dared to consider. Worse still would be to abandon it in the garbage, for somehow the school *maitresse* will discover this ultimate sin and bear news of it to my teta, much to God's outrage. "*Allah 'atena akel ya te'breene, fee gheirna 'am b jou'o*"—"God has blessed us with food, others are starving."

These are my earliest memories of food, and the fear of my teta's wrath, which is a very plausible reason as to why my plate is never given a second to entertain a crumb.

The crumbs that led me to the kitchen

At home in Beirut, we could always expect a soul-stirring rendition from the seasons' star characters as they rehearsed on the stovetop before asserting themselves center stage on our beige, checked, foldable kitchen table. Our meals consisted of many of the quintessentially Lebanese homecooked dishes, from the basic to the intricate. My teta's social foundation schedule, as active as olive oil in a Lebanese kitchen, meant certain days would be reserved for simpler dishes like *mujadarah*, *musaqa'a* or *mutabaqa*. Mutabaqa, meaning "layered" in this instance, is a Lebanese relative of ratatouille, and was sometimes made too often for my jeddo's palate. It often triggered the complaint, "*Taba'te 'a albna ya mara*"—"You've caved in our hearts with this dish woman." Playing on one of the several meanings derived from the root word *tabaqa*, it was a coy effort to express his underwhelmed appetite.

Regardless of what was on the table, though, as the clock struck noon, you could count on my grandfather to stroll over from his nearby law office every day of his married life. Lunch over, he would listen to the news on his radio, read a book or do some writing before his dreams hijacked him into a gentle afternoon siesta.

On Saturday mornings or during school vacations, I would shadow my teta as she went about her grocery shopping. First, we would whiz over to Hanna *al laham* (Hanna the butcher); both his body and his store still strong and upright, their facades evidence of time's great pilgrimage. "*Ahlan b sit Adla,*"—"Welcome our lady Adla," he would greet her, a prelude to a short exchange of words about the well-being of each other's families before the serious business of shopping began, signaled by Hanna's request, "*O'moreené ya sitna*"—"Your orders, Madame." In her stern voice, bereft of hesitation, teta would question the meat's source and time of slaughter. "*Bta'refné ya Hanna ma be'bal gheir b ahsan shee.*"—"You know me, Hanna, I am only satisfied with the best."

At the greengrocer, she would shamelessly bury her hands right to the bottom of the vegetable pile, pulling out several contenders before picking the most worthy. In no way would she be outsmarted by the grocer's conspiracy to keep the older vegetables most exposed. Tomatoes would get a full, twirling, close-up inspection as though they were a model at a casting. Eggplants would be fondled to test their tenderness, and often tossed back in disappointment. On bad mornings, I would hear her discontented muttering: "*Te'te'te, shou hal bda'a ya Rizkallah! Ndahle bas yejeek ahsan!*"—"Such terrible quality of produce! Give me a ring when you get better!" she would announce, before turning on her heel and marching me out of the shop.

Cherished gifts from the land

I was four years old when my parents separated. Born in Houston, I returned to Lebanon with my father, while my siblings remained in the United States with my mother; it was a long time before we would all rendezvous again.

My mother was a beautiful, all-American Texan with golden blonde hair, shimmering, ocean-blue eyes and eyelashes that, when fluttered, could get her into Fort Knox. My Lebanese father was tall, robust and olive skinned, with large, piercing eyes. A hard-working, handsome, 20-something lawyer meant I spent most of my time soaking up the attention of my grandparents. My long, lean and imposing jeddo, with his chiseled cheekbones and a smile that, even in memory, can still light up my heart, was a renowned lawyer and author across the Arab world. His was a fascinating story of hard work, triumph and unmatched determination, deserving every blotch of ink on the flickering pages of Lebanon's history books. "His presence could shake a room," was something I often heard said about him. My grandmother, born to the only commercial tobacco farmer in Lebanon at the time, grew up along the shores of the northern town of Batroun. Stern and articulate, she never missed a beat, and it was said she could read a person and their motives in the glimpse of an eye. Family was the central focus of our life and I was always surrounded by the people who played a pivotal role in my upbringing: my grandparents, aunts and uncles.

My mother returned to Lebanon for a little while with my sisters in tow, and, as the civil war grew with fury and pain, we entrenched ourselves in our ancestral village of Baskinta, in the foothills of Mt. Sannine. My father set up a dairy farm where we spent the next five years embracing the land, its bounty, its unpredictable nature and the general, all-around, rugged goodness.

During the summers, my sisters and I would run in the terraces, hide in the pine forest, explore caves, swing from trees and compete to see who could jump the highest. Quite often, we were bribed to water the orchards, make cheese and help to bring in the harvest in exchange for an allowance that we squandered on junk food, usually a Snickers bar and a Pepsi. My idea of fun was to set up store just outside the house, my toy wagon overflowing with seasonal produce: corn, chickpeas, apples, anything I could sell to ghostly foot traffic. Needless to say, my only customer was my jeddo.

In the autumn, my father and grandmother, would make jam, tomato puree, ketchup, apple cider vinegar, pickles and other *mouneh*, or preserves. My siblings and I would often help with the shelling of the pine nuts and the chickpeas. If the chickpeas were harvested while they were still green, we enjoyed them like sugarsnap peas, otherwise they were left a little longer to wither, then laid out to dry on the roof. Once dry, we would all join together, stepping and grinding to split the pods and release the seeds. The results of our labors were stored in the mouneh room, a full-sized chamber dedicated to the winter's provisions.

We surrendered our appetites to the supremacy of the land and the generous array of ingredients it would gift to us. No matter how dire the situation in our war-torn country, our kitchen table always remained plentiful—a representation not of my father's pocket, but rather his appetite and zeal for life. So it was in the mountains of Lebanon that my connection with the land and with the food that came from it was truly nurtured.

The peal of Taco Bell

By the age of ten, I suddenly found myself back in Houston with my mother, newly born brother and sisters, meeting another side of my family that I had only heard of or seen in pictures. In the United States, I learned to befriend Taco Bell, Wendy's and Jack in the Box. I fell in love with Campbell's soup (the mushroom imposter one, to be precise), SpaghettiOs and Ramen noodle soup.

The few wholesome dishes I can remember eating were a rocking bowl of chili and some sizzling, hickory-smoked ribs my grandfather would make every so often. Of course, there was always Thanksgiving dinner, but even then, the green bean casserole was made straight from the can. My mother's exhaustive work schedule meant she had less time to cook for us, but when she did, she relished making any of the Lebanese dishes she'd picked up from my father, grandmother and aunts. Often, she would treat us to a meal at the local Greek restaurant, which was the next best thing. And so, in many ways and like a spinning globe, my life had been flipped upside down, if food is any good indicator.

Home is where the belly is

My raging appetite for home steered me back to Lebanon once again. By now the 15-year-long civil war in Lebanon was blown out like a trick candle and the country was trying to rebuild itself.

My French and Arabic had been temporarily buried away and I had become a born-again American. A vain teenager by now, I was completely preoccupied with calories and dizzied with the task of reducing my intake of fat to zero, if I could only figure out how while still chewing food. I consumed countless fat-free fads like a glutton consumes cake.

It wouldn't be long before the unrelenting spoon in my father's hand would rekindle my cravings. Living in Lebanon and spending summers in the south of France, my distant love affair with real, honest food would find its way back to my heart.

Eventually, my siblings followed suit to Lebanon and, as the eldest sister, I was promoted to chief household feeder. It's here that I really began to appreciate my love for cooking and for feeding others. More importantly, though, I discovered a cheap and rewarding form of therapy.

Back Stateside again

Fresh into my twenties, I wandered back Stateside, hoping for a bigger poke at life. I drifted aimlessly, chasing lands with flashing neon signs to nickname home. It took a few extended pitstops in Montreal and Houston before I cozied up in Miami with my British flame, now husband, Chris.

Between finding houses for people to buy, flats to rent and mortgages to sign, I managed to gain a reputation as both a wild child and a snow trader to the Inuit. With a heavy workload ahead, I would spend long, therapeutic Saturdays cooking the foods of my homeland, not just to nourish us through the week, but also to satiate the longing. As I whisked, chopped and stirred, as I smelled, tasted and watched others savor each bite, I could fleetingly stumble across that comfortable feeling of belonging. Barbecues were alight nearly every weekend; stray friends, relentless sunshine and unceasing home-cooked Lebanese food meant we almost had it all figured out. And it was during those days in Miami that the idea of a cookbook came to exist, one day in my retirement.

As time passed, we moved on to the even sunnier shores of Maui, Hawaii, where I managed Lahaina Store Grill and Oyster Bar. Chained to the gates of a 500-seater restaurant, I gained force (and weight) by eating island-sized portions of oysters, tuna (poke) and seafood chowder.

But Island Fever would soon catch up with Chris and me, chucking us into the chills of London on an early February morning. Between the aching temperature drop, a brand new culture and a very naked wardrobe, I struggled to brace myself against the screeching and howling winds of change. So, I cooked and I cooked, because that was all that made sense, and here I am now writing that cookbook but not yet retired.

Aromas drifting from the past

The Middle East cradles an ancient cuisine; one of the oldest in the world. It is a cuisine engraved in the tablets of history, although foreign policies, the clash of civilizations and a concern to travel to the region, have kept it but a whisper beneath the dust.

Of course, that's not to downplay a much-deserved tribute to pioneering cookery writers who have championed the cuisine of this region, most notably Claudia Roden, Paula Wolfert, Charles Perry, Arto Der Haroutunian, Anissa Helou, Najmeh Batmanglij and Margaret Shaida. The cuisines, however, have not yet achieved the celebratory recognition of the food of France, Italy, Spain, India or China.

Set the clock back several hundred years, and there was a time in Europe when Middle Eastern food was more than trendy. During the Middle Ages, Islam was the most advanced civilization in the world, contributing vastly to the advancement of Europe in the spheres of science, technology, medicine, art, architecture and food. Over time, with Muslim expansionism and the Crusaders' travels to the Holy Lands, trade expanded and flourished, and spices and exotic ingredients flowed along the Spice Routes, greatly influencing the European palate. Plum pudding, gingerbread, coffee, almond paste, rice pudding, cinnamon, nutmeg and saffron can all be traced through the pages of old cookbooks.

Over the last decade, meze has settled well on Western dining room tables, and almost everyone knows its main ambassadors: hummus, tabbouleh and grape leaves. But there still exists a vast and distinct culinary heritage that remains unexplored: wholesome stews, exotic casseroles and a range of domestic cooking that routinely welcomes home hungry school children and soothes the appetites of tired workers. These are the dishes that feed the peasants and the affluent alike, and many are dishes that have drifted in straight from the past.

Culinary footprints

With Arabic being the predominant language of the territories that make up the Middle East, most dishes across the region share the same name, with their diversity concealed in the seasonings and preparation methods. This also lends a friendly culinary rivalry between the countries of the region, where the few dishes that are specialities of a particular country become integral to its national identity. Take *musakhan*, for example. While popular in both Palestine and Jordan, ask a Palestinian and they will swear it's their own culinary treasure.

Middle Eastern food has also been influenced by visiting cultures, as peoples from both East and West have danced and mingled on Middle Eastern soil, each leaving behind a footprint from its own tradition without troubling the fundamental flavors. For example, Persian, Iraqi and Gulf cuisines share many similarities and, while they also show traces of Mediterranean influences, they are, in particular, more abundant in meat, overflowing with rice dishes, and have taken much of their use of spices from India.

The Mediterranean cuisines of Turkey, Lebanon, Syria, Palestine, Jordan and North Africa use prolific amounts of pulses, grains, nuts, citrus fruits, garlic, fresh herbs, allspice and to some extent olive oil.

Eating the Middle Eastern way

In a Middle Eastern kitchen, fresh ingredients are celebrated in tune with the seasons or conserved as part of the ritual of preservation; simple yet clever. Real home-style dishes revolve around humble vegetables and grains, which are used to extend the limited amounts of meat that might be available. While an abundance of invigorating spices prevail in the cuisine, heat for the most part does not dwell in it. Exceptions can be found in some of the dishes of North Africa, Turkey, Palestine and Yemen.

Garlic, lemon and fresh herbs feature heavily and there is an affectionate respect for marrying sweet and sour tones with the use of verjuice, pomegranate molasses and citrus fruit. Yogurt is enjoyed on its own, as labneh, or as an integral part of many dishes—so much so it's difficult to imagine this cuisine without it. Of even more significance, though, is the use of bread. Not only nutritional, it's served with every meal, however humble or lavish, and used interchangeably with or even replacing silverware (for most in the region, eating many of the dishes without bread to mop up the juices is inconceivable). Moreover, it's also considered a gift from God, to be cherished and honored. So intricate to the culture is bread, and the ritual surrounding its breaking, that a well-known proverb demonstrates the intimacy and unbreakable bonds of friendship it represents: "there is bread and salt between us."

The generous table

Religion and landscape have contributed to the strict notions of hospitality in the Middle East, lavishing this ancient culture with virtues, customs and overwhelming etiquettes. A Middle Eastern meal is a titilating contradiction to the rigid, three-course Western meal. In fact, it begins well before anyone sits down at the table. Guests are always greeted with tea and a selection of dried fruit, nuts and pastries to unfasten their appetite for the real feast.

The meal that follows is relaxed and fluid and, depending on location and social class, diners might gather around either a table or a *sofrah*, which may be as simple as a cloth laid out on the floor. The table is adorned like a glistening Byzantine empress, with a wide variety of dishes, served in a quick procession. Guests use bread instead of silverware to scoop up food from the communal dishes or from their own plates. One can expect to be urged toward second and third helpings, so a wise diner eats less on the first helping. The more you eat, the more pleasure and pride your host experiences, feeling they have done their job well in taking good care of you. Desserts are not usually eaten after a meal, although guests might enjoy fresh fruits and sweet pastries with their tea. This overwhelming generosity is not only the preserve of the wealthy; genuine hospitality is shown right across the social scale, sometimes even beyond a family's means.

A culinary marriage

Growing up, I repeatedly heard my father quote the Chinese philosopher, Confucius: "Study the past if you would define the future." This would become a philosophy to which I prescribe, especially when contemplating Middle Eastern cuisine. I am as fascinated by the history of our cuisine, its ancient recipes, techniques and rituals, as I am by the new and wonderful dishes it can inspire.

This philosophy, though, is not always welcome when approaching such a deep-rooted cuisine. More than once, I have come up against relatives who have challenged the most miniscule alteration I have made to a dish, outraged by the fact that I dared to call it by the same name. "This is not how you make *moghrabieh*!" "No, no, you cannot put cumin in *kebbeh*! What, are you crazy?" You see, although Middle Eastern and North African culinary traditions celebrate an abundance of regional variations that have been passed down over the years without precise measurements, each family and each village has become chained to its own set beliefs.

A few brave chefs have begun dabbling with modern Middle Eastern cuisine, among them Greg Malouf, although this is still a fairly new concept. The result is that we now have a large blank canvas to begin working on, and this is what excites me: cooking the foods of my childhood while knowing that there is a vast expanse of wonder and innovation to look forward to. All we need to do is to grasp the opportunity without fear or hesitation. We are not disrespecting our past or our traditions but, rather, admiring where they have brought us and, when coupled with our present, where they might lead us.

The jeweled kitchen

Developing the recipes for my first book has been both a revelation of the Middle Eastern and North African culinary traditions and a tantalizing glimpse at the possibilities that lie ahead. I like to think of this book as an ode to the treasured dishes of the past, embracing a creative and contemporary approach. I hope it will ignite (and feed) your curiosity as it has inspired and excited my own.

Over the following chapters you'll find ideas for marvelous meze, poultry, meat, seafood and vegetarian dishes. Some of these beautiful dishes can be thrown together from scratch in a matter of minutes, while more ambitious dishes are made easy with clear directions and clever cooking techniques.

I have also indulged the sweet tooth of my childhood to tempt you with recipes for irresistible desserts and delicate pastries. The final chapter will help you master the cornerstones of the cuisine, with recipes for breads, dips, condiments, spice mixes, stocks, cheese and pastry, as well as advice on how to prepare and cook rice and chickpeas perfectly.

With this book you can explore the Persian love of herbs and fragrance, the hearty and comforting dishes of the Mediterranean and the rich variety of ingredients celebrated by the cuisines of the Gulf, as you turn humble ingredients into a beguiling array of spectacular, contemporary dishes.

The Middle Eastern & North African pantry

All of the authentic ingredients used in this book are readily available online or from specialist grocers, but you might feel unsure about using some of the more exotic ingredients such as *mahlab* or Aleppo pepper. Don't worry. The glossary at the back of the book will help you learn more about how to source, prepare and store any unfamiliar ingredients, as well as suggesting suitable alternatives.

It's always best to use high-quality ingredients. Remember, too, all ingredients are not born alike. A tomato in Texas will taste entirely different from one in, say, Lebanon, and that can really affect the harmony of a tomato-based stew. An eggplant you purchased this week can taste very different from the one you enjoyed two weeks ago. The length of time your spice has been sitting on the shelf will, more or less, determine the quantity required, as its potency reduces over time. And then there is the fluctuating taste of lemons, some more acidic than others, while some of us have more or less tolerance for sour flavors. And let's not forget the level of spice: if you are not an avid lover of spicy food and a dish sounds like it's going to be too hot, reduce the quantity of spices and adjust as you cook. It's all a matter of taste.

The breath of inspiration

Recipes, elaborate instructions, precise measurements; this is the stuff that fumbles me. For while I am very aware many do not feel comfortable without these specifics, I become stifled, flustered in my own domain, stumbling as I try to stay true to a recipe.

Middle Eastern recipes are passed down over the centuries, most often from mother to daughter or within the female community, but precise weights and measures are rarely part of the instruction. A large spoonful of this, an Arabic coffee cup of that, a squeeze of lemon, just enough water ... these are the units of measure in a Middle Eastern kitchen, with the emphasis on constant tasting and adjustment.

In the Middle East and North Africa, cooking truly is an instinctive art form. In the Middle East we say a good cook has *nafas* which, directly translated, means "breath," but when used in the context of cooking means "flair;" for there is an association with the sense of smell, too—of inspiration.

Although I have given precise measurements throughout, nothing is rigid or set in stone (baking aside). So rather than slavishly using scales or measuring jugs instead rely on the most powerful tools at your disposal: your senses. Listen to the bubbling liquid, look at the vibrant colours, feel the texture but, above all, smell the aromas and taste your dish as you cook—you can't taste too much. Only then will you be able to see if your meal needs more nurturing or if it just wants to be left alone.

Whether you are cooking for your immediate family or a crowd of friends, the objective is to create an enjoyable meal that evokes comfort and happiness. As you've heard many others say, cooking is meant to be fun, not serious. Run with your senses and, most importantly, enjoy yourself.

Cooking and eating are among life's greatest pleasures, and as my uncle always says to me, "*Kelé w nsee hammeek*" – "Eat and you shall forget your worries."

meze

Silky Chickpea & Lamb Soup

SERVES 4
PREPARATION TIME: 30 minutes,
  plus soaking the chickpeas, making
  the starter (optional) and making
  the stock and preserved lemon
COOKING TIME: 1½ hours, plus
  cooking the chickpeas until tender
  (optional)

2 tablespoons rye flour (optional)

2 tablespoons white bread flour
  (optional)

12 ounces lamb shank

¼ teaspoon ground cardamom

¼ teaspoon ground cumin

¼ teaspoon smoked paprika

¼ teaspoon ground coriander

¼ teaspoon ground cinnamon

1½ pounds tomatoes

4 teaspoons salted butter or smen

1 onion, finely chopped

4 garlic cloves, roughly chopped

2-inch piece gingerroot, peeled and
  finely chopped

8¾ cups Vegetable Stock (see page
  211)

a pinch ground saffron (optional)

½ cup dried chickpeas, soaked
  overnight and cooked (see page
  215), or 1 cup canned chickpeas,
  drained and rinsed

1¼ cups brown lentils, rinsed

1 bay leaf

1 wedge Preserved Lemon (see
  page 212), peel rinsed and finely
  chopped, or zest of ½ lemon

1 tablespoon finely chopped cilantro
  leaves, plus extra for sprinkling

sea salt and ground black pepper

a few pitted dates, to serve

1 lemon, quartered, to squeeze

warm Arabic Bread (optional, see
  page 217), to serve

During the holy month of Ramadan, in North Africa, this silky textured soup is the first dish with which the fast is broken. It goes well with Pan-Fried Squares (see page 149).

1 If you are using the starter, which will give a thicker, smoother soup, early in the morning two days in advance, put 2 teaspoons of the rye flour and 2 teaspoons bread flour in a mixing bowl and mix together. Pour 1 tablespoon lukewarm water over and mix well, then cover with paper towels. Set the starter aside somewhere warm (72° to 77°F).

2 During the morning of the following day, "feed" the starter with the remaining flours and about 2 teaspoons lukewarm water, stirring very well to combine. Set aside, covered as above, 8 hours longer.

3 Rub the lamb shank with the cardamom, cumin, smoked paprika, coriander and cinnamon and season with salt. Set aside.

4 With a sharp knife, cut a cross in the skin of each tomato, then put them in a heatproof bowl and cover with boiling water. Leave them to stand 2 to 3 minutes or until the skins split, then drain. Plunge into cold water to stop them cooking, then peel off the skins and discard. Slice each tomato in half and scoop out the seeds, then finely chop the flesh.

5 Melt the butter in a heavy-bottomed saucepan over medium heat. Add the onion, cover the pan and reduce the heat to low, then leave to sweat, stirring often, 5 minutes, or until soft.

6 Increase the heat to medium, add the lamb and any loose spices and sear 3 minutes on each side. Add the garlic and ginger and cook 1 minute longer, or until aromatic. Add the tomatoes, stock, saffron, if using, cooked chickpeas, the lentils and bay leaf.

7 Cover the pan, increase the heat to high and bring to a boil, then reduce the heat to medium-low and simmer, covered, 1 hour, or until the lentils are soft and the meat is tender. Discard the bay leaf.

8 Remove the lamb from the pan and cut the meat into bite-size pieces, then return the meat to the pan with the bone. The marrow can be extracted with a narrow spoon or skewer, if wanted.

9 Dilute the starter, if using, with 7 tablespoons water, stir well, then slowly pour it into the pan, stirring about 20 minutes until the mixture becomes thicker. Stir in the preserved lemon and cilantro and season to taste with pepper. Ladle into bowls, sprinkle with extra cilantro and serve with dates, lemon quarters and with warm Arabic Bread, if liked.

tuna tartare with chermoula

SERVES 4
PREPARATION TIME: 45 minutes,
   plus making the preserved lemon
   and grinding the saffron
COOKING TIME: 5 minutes

7 tablespoons salted butter

1 egg white, beaten

1 tablespoon honey

5 sheets phyllo pastry dough,
   thawed if frozen

¼ cup sesame seeds

3 tablespoons Greek yogurt

¼ teaspoon ground saffron
   (optional, see page 212) or turmeric

1 wedge Preserved Lemon
   (see page 212), peel rinsed

10 ounces sushi-grade yellowfin
   tuna, salmon or scallops,
   well chilled

FOR THE CHERMOULA

¼ teaspoon cumin seeds

1 handful parsley leaves

1 handful cilantro leaves

2 dill sprigs

1 ¼-inch piece gingerroot, peeled

1 small to medium red chili, seeded
   and roughly chopped

1 fat garlic clove, crushed with the
   blade of a knife

1 wedge Preserved Lemon
   (see page 212), peel rinsed

3 tablespoons olive oil

sea salt and freshly ground black
   pepper

This is inspired by the Hawaiian poke I devoured on a daily basis when managing a restaurant in Maui. If you cannot find tuna, use sushi-grade salmon or scallops. Sear if you prefer.

1 Heat the oven to 375°F. Melt the butter in a small pan, then pour it into a mixing bowl with the egg white, honey and a pinch salt. Whisk until smooth and thick.

2 Remove the sheets of phyllo dough from their packaging and cover them quickly with a damp dish towel. Place one sheet of dough on a cutting board, brush it with a thin layer of the butter mixture, top with a second sheet and brush with more of the butter mixture. Repeat with the remaining phyllo sheets. The edges will crinkle as you position each sheet, and you might need to align them gently with your fingers.

3 Sprinkle the sesame seeds evenly over the top sheet. Using a sharp knife or pastry wheel, cut the layered phyllo in half lengthwise, then slice down the sheet every 4 inches, creating eight rectangles. Cut each rectangle diagonally in half. Carefully transfer the triangles to two cookie sheets and bake 4 to 5 minutes until golden brown. Transfer to a plate lined with paper towels to cool.

4 Meanwhile, to make the chermoula, toast the cumin seeds in a heavy-bottomed pan over medium heat 1 to 2 minutes until fragrant, shaking the pan often. Transfer to a small food processor, add the parsley, cilantro, dill, ginger, chili, garlic and preserved lemon wedge, and pulse until it combines to form a fine paste. Drizzle in the oil and season with salt, then pulse to combine.

5 Put the yogurt in a separate bowl and add the saffron, if using, and salt to taste. Whisk with a hand blender until frothy. Finely chop the lemon wedge and stir it in.

6 Using a sharp, thin-bladed knife and a very clean cutting board, slice the tuna into ½-inch cubes. Divide the tuna into eight equal portions. Place a metal pastry ring about 2 inches in diameter in the middle of a plate, spoon in about 1 teaspoon of the yogurt sauce, then 1 portion of the tuna, 1 teaspoon of the chermoula sauce and then another portion of the tuna. Drizzle 1 teaspoon of the yogurt sauce over. Repeat with the remaining ingredients to make 4 servings. Season with salt and pepper and top each stack with 4 phyllo triangles.

artichokes with couscous

SERVES 4
PREPARATION TIME: 30 minutes,
  plus making the stock and jam
  (optional)
COOKING TIME: 1 hour

½ cup couscous

1 tablespoon butter

3 ½ cups Vegetable Stock (see
  page 211)

4 fresh artichokes or 4 brined
  artichoke hearts

1 lemon, halved

4 garlic cloves, finely chopped

8 small anchovy fillets in oil, drained
  and roughly chopped

8 olives, pitted and roughly chopped

2 teaspoons capers, drained and
  rinsed

2 tablespoons Burned Tomato &
  Chili Jam (see page 219) or finely
  chopped tomatoes

1 tablespoon finely chopped mint
  leaves, to sprinkle

sea salt and freshly ground black
  pepper

This dish offers something for everyone. It's perfect if you want to knock something up very quickly, in which case you can use brined artichoke hearts and instant couscous. Otherwise, it's a great way to use fresh artichokes in season, which makes for longer, but very rewarding, cooking.

1 Put the couscous in a bowl, add the butter and rub it into the couscous. Line the top half of a steamer with cheesecloth and put the buttered couscous in the steamer basket. Pour the vegetable stock into the bottom half and place over medium heat. Once the stock comes to a boil, place the steamer basket over it, cover and steam 30 minutes, or until the couscous is soft. Reserve any remaining stock.

2 Meanwhile, to prepare the artichoke hearts, begin by cutting off the stem close to the bottom and then peeling off the outer leaves of each artichoke, either one-by-one or pulling off a few at a time (not too many, though, or you'll tear into the fleshy bottom). The leaves will get softer and smaller as you progress, and then you'll reach the fuzzy choke. Using a spoon or a paring knife, gently scrape out all the inner choke to leave a bowl-shaped cavity. You don't want any of the prickly hairs to remain. Quickly squeeze one of the lemon halves onto the artichoke hearts to prevent them from browning, then transfer them to a bowl filled with ⸻ ⸻nd the juice of the remaining lemon half. Alternatively, if using brined artichoke hearts, rinse the brined hearts well and place in a bowl of water with a squeeze of lemon.

3 Toss the steamed couscous with the garlic, anchovies, olives, capers and jam. Season lightly with salt (the anchovies will already have made the dish salty) and pepper. Fill the cavity in each artichoke heart with the couscous mixture. Stand the artichokes in a large, heavy-bottomed saucepan and pour the reserved stock over (diluted with more water if there isn't enough: the stock should come to just below the top of the artichokes). Cover partially and cook over medium heat 30 minutes, or until the artichoke hearts are soft. Serve warm, sprinkled with mint.

mixed greens frittata

SERVES 4
PREPARATION TIME: 15 minutes,
 plus making the advieh
COOKING TIME: 20 minutes

1 tablespoon dried barberries or
 cranberries (optional)

2 tablespoons finely chopped
 parsley leaves

2 tablespoons finely chopped
 cilantro leaves

2 tablespoons finely chopped
 tarragon leaves

2 tablespoons finely chopped
 dill leaves

2 tablespoons finely snipped chives

8 eggs

1 teaspoon baking powder

1 teaspoon Advieh 2 (see page 211)

3 tablespoons salted butter, of which
 1 tablespoon is soft and diced

1 tablespoon chopped walnuts
 (optional)

⅓ cup feta, crumbled

sea salt and freshly ground black
 pepper

TO SERVE
warm Thin Flatbread (see page 218)

lime wedges

Greek yogurt

side salad (optional)

dried edible rose petals, crumbled
 (optional)

This recipe is loosely based on kookoo sabzi ("kookoo" implies the use of an egg and "sabzi" means mixed greens), which is the most popular of all the Persian kookoos. An abundant and almost frivolous mix of herbs and vegetables, it's served during Nowruz, the Persian New Year festivities, and symbolizes new beginnings. Both the barberries and walnuts are optional, and are usually reserved for special occasions.

1 Put the barberries, if using, in a small bowl of water and leave to soak 5 minutes, then drain. Use paper towels to pat out as much moisture as you can from the soaked barberries and the herbs.

2 Whisk the eggs vigorously in a large bowl with the baking powder, advieh, soft butter, herbs, barberries and walnuts, if using, and season with salt and pepper.

3 Melt the remaining butter in a nonstick skillet with a flameproof handle over high heat. When the butter begins to foam, pour in the egg and herb mixture and stir well, then reduce the heat and cook 15 minutes, or until well risen and almost fully set on top. Sprinkle with the feta. Meanwhile, heat the broiler to high.

4 Place the pan under the broiler and broil about 5 minutes until the frittata is set on the top and just cooked through.

5 Transfer the frittata to a plate and sprinkle with dried rose petals, if you like. Serve immediately with warm Thin Flatbread, lime wedges and yogurt. Alternatively, leave to cool and enjoy as a light snack with a simple salad.

spinach & sumac turnovers

SERVES 4
PREPARATION TIME: 40 minutes,
  plus making the pastry dough
COOKING TIME: 10 minutes

2¾ ounces spinach leaves or Swiss
  chard

1 teaspoon sea salt

1 small onion, finely chopped (scant
  ½ cup)

2 tablespoons sumac

1 teaspoon ground allspice

2 tablespoons olive oil, plus extra
  for greasing

a pinch dried chili flakes (optional)

2 tablespoons pine nuts

all-purpose flour, for dusting

1 recipe quantity Savory Pastry
  Dough (see page 213)

The key to achieving dainty turnovers is to make the dough slightly wet and the filling dry. Practice by making larger ones first. The balance between onion and spinach is vital for success, which is why I've included the onion's cup measure.

1 Wash the spinach and pat it dry, then chop finely. Put the spinach in a bowl and sprinkle with ½ teaspoon of the salt, then rub it all together very well until the spinach breaks down and water starts to drain out. Leave to rest about 5 minutes, then squeeze the spinach tightly to remove the liquid. Do this very well to make sure all the juice is expelled, otherwise sealing the turnovers will be a difficult task.

2 Put the onion in another bowl and sprinkle with the remaining salt, then rub it well 1 to 2 minutes until it is soft. Squeeze out any water and then add the onion to the spinach and continue mixing, squeezing out and discarding any excess water until the mixture is dry. Add the sumac, allspice, oil and chili flakes, if using.

3 Toast the pine nuts in a heavy-bottomed pan over medium heat 1 to 2 minutes until golden and fragrant, shaking the pan often. Add to the mixture, then taste and adjust the seasoning, if required, bearing in mind the mixture is meant to be very sour.

4 Heat the oven to 400°F and lightly grease a cookie sheet. Meanwhile, roll out the dough on a well-floured countertop into a large circle about ⅟₁₆ inch thick. If necessary, divide the dough in half and roll it out and stamp it in two stages. For best results, you might find it helps to flip the dough a few times between rolling and sprinkling with more flour.

5 Using a 2¾-inch round cookie cutter, stamp out 20 to 25 circles. Place 1 teaspoon of the stuffing in the middle of each circle and use your thumb and index finger to seal the edges together to form a half-moon shape, but stop once you get halfway. Then, as your thumb and index continue to pinch, use your other hand to bring over the remaining unsealed dough so the edges meet perpendicularly. Seal, and with the help of your index finger, lift the dough at three points, joining them into a triangle with a peak at the joint. Pinch together tightly, and thin out gently until you do not see a crease, so they stay sealed during baking. Check that all the turnovers are firmly sealed. (You can freeze them at this stage in an airtight, freezersafe container up to 2 months).

6 Put the turnovers on the cookie sheet. Bake 7 minutes, or until golden brown and crisp at the edges. Remove from the oven and serve hot or at room temperature.

dynamite chili cigars

SERVES 4
PREPARATION TIME: 30 minutes
COOKING TIME: 10 minutes

olive oil, for greasing

9 ounces soft goat cheese, crumbled

1 garlic clove, finely chopped

1 small mild red chili, seeded and very thinly sliced

2 teaspoons dried oregano

1 teaspoon sesame seeds

1 egg, separated

4 or 5 sheets phyllo pastry dough, thawed if frozen

5 tablespoons salted butter

sea salt and freshly ground black pepper

Known as briwat in Morocco, we have something quite similar in the Levant called raqaqat. What's lovely about this recipe is that there is plenty of cheese and not too much phyllo, so the "cigar" is very creamy, with a light and crisp casing. Some of them might explode a bit in the oven, but this is fine. They are not called "dynamite" for nothing...! These can be assembled up to 4 hours ahead, then covered with plastic wrap and kept in the refrigerator until ready to bake.

1 Heat the oven to 350°F and lightly grease a baking sheet with oil. Put the crumbled goat cheese, garlic, chili, oregano, sesame seeds and egg yolk in a mixing bowl and beat well. Season to taste with salt and pepper.

2 Remove 4 sheets of the phyllo from their packaging and cut into 7- x 4-inch strips. You should get 24 strips, depending on how accurately you cut them. If you are short, use part of the last sheet, too. Cover the strips with a damp dish towel to stop the dough drying out while you work.

3 Melt the butter in a small saucepan over low heat. Working with one phyllo strip at a time, and keeping the others covered, place a strip on the countertop with a short end toward you. Brush the strip with melted butter, then put another strip on top and brush that with butter.

4 Place scant 1 tablespoon of the goat cheese filling at the short end nearest to you, leaving ½ inch phyllo on each side. Fold the strip over the filling, and fold in the sides all the way to the end, then roll away from you to form a "cigar."

5 Beat the egg white, then use it to brush the seam and brush all over the phyllo roll with a little more melted butter. Repeat with the remaining ingredients to make 12 rolls in total.

6 Put the cigars seam-side down on the prepared baking sheet and bake 5 to 7 minutes until light golden and crisp. Serve hot.

red-hot roasties

SERVES 4
PREPARATION TIME: 30 minutes
COOKING TIME: 1 ¼ hours

2 ¼ pounds Idaho potatoes, peeled and chopped into 1 ½-inch cubes

1 tablespoon sea salt flakes

1 handful cilantro leaves, finely chopped, plus extra for sprinkling

2 small mild red chilies, seeded and finely chopped

1 garlic bulb, cloves separated and finely chopped

1 teaspoon paprika

⅓ cup olive oil

juice of 1 lemon

freshly ground black pepper

TO SERVE
fried eggs

Spiced Naked Mini Sausages (see page 21)

warm Arabic Bread (optional, see page 217)

I'm a diehard fan of the texture of these spicy roast potatoes. They are my interpretation of the popular meze dish batata harra. For the crispiest results, use floury Idaho or other baking potatoes, rather than waxy ones. Simply serve with fried eggs on top and some Spiced Naked Mini Sausages and Arabic bread.

1 Heat the oven to 400°F. Rinse the potatoes under cold, running water for a few minutes to wash off any surface starch.

2 Bring 4 cups water to a boil in a saucepan over high heat. Add the salt and the potatoes and cook about 5 minutes until the edges of the potato pieces soften.

3 Meanwhile, put the cilantro, chilies, garlic and paprika in a small bowl and mix well. Season to taste with salt and pepper.

4 Drain the potatoes and return to the pan. Stretch a dish towel securely over the top and shake the pan about 30 seconds until the edges of the potatoes fluff up. Set aside, uncovered, to let all the moisture evaporate.

5 Meanwhile, brush a 9 ½- x 12-inch roasting pan with the oil, then place the pan in the oven about 10 minutes until the oil is sizzling hot.

6 Remove the pan from the oven and spoon the potatoes into the sizzling oil, gently turning them so they are well coated. Return the pan to the oven and roast, uncovered, 35 to 40 minutes until light golden brown. Sprinkle the cilantro and garlic mixture over, turning the potatoes to make sure they are well coated. Return the pan to the oven and roast 10 to 15 minutes longer until the potatoes are crisp and golden brown.

7 Remove the pan from the oven and transfer the potatoes to a serving dish. Squeeze the lemon juice over and sprinkle with more cilantro. Serve warm with fried eggs, Spiced Naked Mini Sausages and warm Arabic Bread, if you like.

Shipwrecked potato boats

SERVES 4
PREPARATION TIME: 10 minutes
COOKING TIME: 1 hour 10 minutes

4 large potatoes, halved lengthwise

4 tablespoons olive oil

10 tablespoons (2 ½ sticks) salted butter

3 garlic cloves, crushed or finely chopped

¼ teaspoon ground cumin

1 teaspoon dried coriander

3 tablespoons finely snipped chives

2 teaspoons sesame seeds

sea salt and freshly ground black pepper

Burned Tomato & Chili Jam (see page 219), to serve

These were born of my attempts to deconstruct a potato cake. Here, the essence of fluffy mashed potato is retained, while the crisp crust is reincarnated through the use of the much-neglected potato skin. Use Idaho or other baking potatoes for these. Try the boats with flaked smoked mackerel or allow your imagination to lead you wherever you want. While the cooking time is just more than an hour, the actual active time required to knock these up is about 10 minutes. Baking the potato skins is a suitable alternative if you're steering clear of frying: brush each skin with 1 tablespoon olive oil and bake 10 minutes at the same temperature as the potatoes.

1 Heat the oven to 425°F. Brush the potato halves lightly with a little of the oil. Cover each one with foil and seal the packages tightly. Place them directly on the oven rack or on a baking sheet and bake about 1 hour until the flesh is soft. Remove the potatoes from the oven and leave 5 minutes, or until cool enough to handle, then scoop out the flesh into a mixing bowl.

2 Heat the remaining oil in a skillet over medium heat and fry the potato skins 2 to 3 minutes each side until they are crisp, then transfer them to a plate lined with paper towels.

3 Add the butter, garlic, cumin and coriander to the potato flesh and season to taste with salt and pepper. Using a potato masher or ricer, mash the potatoes until they are light and fluffy and do not have any lumps, but don't mash for too long or they will be overworked and gluey. Sprinkle the chives over and mix just enough to combine. Spoon the mixture equally into the potato skins. If the mashed potatoes cool too much during this process, and are difficult to spoon, just transfer to the still-warm oven a couple of minutes.

4 Toast the sesame seeds in a heavy-bottomed pan over medium heat 1 minute, or until golden and fragrant, shaking the pan often. Sprinkle them over the stuffed potatoes. Serve with some Burned Tomato and Chili Jam.

Corn-on-the-kobab
with pistachio-saffron butter

SERVES 4
PREPARATION TIME: 15 minutes
COOKING TIME: 12 minutes

sunflower oil, for greasing

½ teaspoon saffron threads

6 tablespoons unsalted butter,
  slightly soft

4 garlic cloves, roughly chopped

1 tablespoon shelled pistachios

4 corn cobs

2 tablespoons sea salt, plus extra
  for seasoning

freshly ground black pepper

lime wedges, to serve

Dunking corn in hot, salted water after barbecuing it makes a delicious departure from the usual boiled corn.

1 Depending on your choice, heat a charcoal barbecue until the charcoal is burning white or turn on a gas barbecue to high. Lightly grease the rack with oil.

2 Toast the saffron threads in a heavy-bottomed skillet over medium heat a few seconds, or until fragrant, then tip them into a small food processor with the butter and garlic. Season to taste with salt and pepper. Pulse about 1 minute until the butter is smooth. Transfer the butter to a serving dish.

3 Put the pistachios in the skillet and toast over medium heat 1 to 2 minutes until light brown, then crush using a mortar and pestle. Sprinkle the crushed pistachios over the flavored butter and stir to incorporate. Set aside until ready to use.

4 Peel off the corn husks, remove all the silky threads and rinse the cobs well under cold running water.

5 Place the corn cobs on the barbecue and cook about 10 minutes until tender and lightly charred, turning them every few minutes so they cook evenly. Corn cooks quickly, so keep an eye on it. You'll hear the corn kernels popping—that's normal. If you want to cook the corn on a gas stovetop, simply turn the flame to medium and lean the corn against the flame, turning with tongs every minute or so, and cook 4 to 5 minutes.

6 While the corn is cooking, put the salt in a wide, heatproof bowl large enough for dunking all the corn at once. Add 4¼ cups hot water to the bowl and stir to dissolve the salt.

7 Once the corn is cooked, use tongs to remove the cobs from the barbecue and submerge them in the hot water a few seconds, then remove. The water will evaporate quickly. Cut the cobs in half and insert corn holders at the ends of the halves, then roll and rub them in the pistachio-saffron butter, covering them generously. Serve with lime wedges.

Jeweled rice

SERVES 4
PREPARATION TIME: 30 minutes,
  plus making the rice, advieh and
  saffron liquid
COOKING TIME: 35 minutes

¼ cup dried currants

1 cup dried barberries or cranberries

1 bitter orange, such as a Seville

¾ cup slivered almonds

½ cup shelled pistachios, halved

1 tablespoon finely chopped
  mint leaves

5 tablespoons sunflower oil

1 recipe quantity Parboiled Rice (see
  pages 214)

1 teaspoon Advieh 2 (see page 211)

4 tablespoons unsalted butter

2 tablespoons Saffron Liquid (see
  page 212)

*The berries, nuts and dried fruit mirror the effect of precious
stones in this dish, with its elaborate layers of texture.*

1 Soak the currants in a bowl of water 10 minutes, or until swollen. Put
the barberries in a separate bowl of water and soak 5 minutes. Drain
both and pat dry separately. Set aside.

2 Peel the orange, removing all the pith. Cut the peel into thin julienne
strips, then transfer to a small saucepan. Pour enough cold water
to cover over, bring to a boil and blanch 20 seconds, then drain. Repeat
the blanching twice more to remove any bitterness.

3 Reserve 1 tablespoon each of the slivered almonds, pistachios and
soaked currants and combine the remainder with the blanched orange
strips, then mix in the mint. Set aside.

4 Heat the oil in a heavy-bottomed saucepan over medium heat until
it is sizzling. Using a spoon, sprinkle 4 to 5 tablespoons of the rice across
the bottom to cover. Sprinkle 1 tablespoon of the fruit and nut mixture
over the top, then sprinkle in a pinch advieh. Continue adding layers
of rice, the fruit and nut mixture and the advieh, building the mixture
up into a dome. Finish with a layer of rice. Avoid tipping all the rice
in at once, because this will compress it and the result will not be light.

5 Using the handle of a wooden spoon, make three holes in the rice all
the way to the bottom of the pan. This forms the tahdeeg, or crisp base.

6 Melt half the butter in a small pan. Add the saffron liquid and
2 tablespoons water and mix well. Pour the mixture over the rice.

7 Wrap the saucepan lid in a clean dish towel and tie it into a tight
knot at the handle, then use it to cover the pan as tightly as you can
so the steam does not escape. (The dish towel prevents the moisture
from dripping into the rice, making it soggy.) Cook the rice over
medium heat 2 to 3 minutes until it is steaming (you will see puffs
of steam escaping at the edges of the lid), then reduce the heat to low
and cook, covered, 20 to 25 minutes.

8 Meanwhile, melt the remaining butter in a small heavy-bottomed
saucepan over medium heat, add the soaked barberries and fry, stirring
often, 3 to 4 minutes to refresh their color. Remove the pan from the
heat and set aside for serving.

9 Serve the rice and tahdeeg following the directions in steps 5–7 for
Steamed Rice on page 214. Decorate the rice with the reserved slivered
almonds, pistachios and soaked currants and also the soaked barberries.

warm hummus in a cumin & olive oil broth

SERVES 4
PREPARATION TIME: 15 minutes,
  plus soaking the chickpeas
  (optional)
COOKING TIME: 30 minutes, plus
  cooking the chickpeas until they
  are very tender (optional)

2 cups dried chickpeas, soaked
  overnight and cooked (see page
  215), or 4 cups canned chickpeas,
  drained and rinsed

2 garlic cloves, finely chopped

1 teaspoon cumin, plus extra
  to sprinkle

5 tablespoons olive oil, plus extra
  to drizzle

2 tablespoons pine nuts

1 tablespoon chopped parsley
  leaves, to sprinkle

sea salt

TO SERVE
warm Arabic Bread (see page 217)

Fattoush Salad (see page 61)

Spinach & Sumac Turnovers
  (see page 37)

Yogurt, Cucumber & Mint Salad
  (see page 66)

Spiced Naked Mini Sausages
  (optional, see page 21)

This comforting winter vegetarian dish, called hummus balila, is served warm. Served with Spiced Naked Mini Sausages (see page 21 or chorizo it also makes a robust, nonvegetarians main course. Allspice can be used if cumin is too powerful a flavor for you.

1 Strain the cooked chickpeas, reserving about ½ cup of the cooking liquid. Put the chickpeas in a heavy-bottomed saucepan with the reserved liquid and garlic. If using canned chickpeas, replace the reserved cooking liquid with water.

2 Heat over medium heat and stir to combine, then bring to a gentle boil. Once boiling, reduce the heat to low and season to taste with salt, then sprinkle in the cumin and mix well. Cook 2 to 3 minutes longer, then remove the pan from the heat. Pour in the oil and set aside, covered. Some of the chickpeas might have disintegrated, creating a thick, saucelike texture. This adds to the richness of the dish, but you still want the majority of the chickpeas to remain whole. Transfer the chickpea mixture into a meze-style serving bowl.

3 Toast the pine nuts in a heavy-bottomed skillet over medium heat 1 to 2 minutes until golden and fragrant, shaking the pan often. Sprinkle the pine nuts and the extra cumin over the chickpea mixture and drizzle extra oil over, if you like. Finally, sprinkle with the chopped parsley. Serve immediately with warm Arabic Bread, Fattoush Salad, Spinach & Sumac Turnovers, Yogurt, Cucumber and Mint Salad and Spiced Naked Mini Sausages, if you like.

swimming chickpeas

SERVES 4
PREPARATION TIME: 30 minutes,
  plus soaking the chickpeas
  (optional) and making
  the tarator
COOKING TIME: cooking the
  chickpeas until they are very soft
  (optional)

1 ¼ cups dried chickpeas, soaked
  overnight and cooked (see
  page 215), or 2 ½ cups canned
  chickpeas, drained and rinsed

½ recipe quantity Tarator (see
  page 220)

5 tablespoons olive oil, to drizzle

½ teaspoon Aleppo pepper flakes
  or crushed chili flakes, to sprinkle

1 tablespoon finely chopped parsley
  leaves, to sprinkle

warm Arabic Bread (optional,
  see page 217), to serve

*The native name for this Syrian dish, hummus musabaha,
derives from the Arabic word sabaha, meaning "to swim."
A traditional breakfast food, the chickpeas are served
"swimming" in a pool of tahini and oodles of olive oil. The dish
incorporates the same ingredients as hummus b tahini, but
they're not whipped into a puree, which gives the dish more
texture and body. Make sure your chickpeas are super-soft:
collapsing at the gentlest touch. I've found removing the skins,
although more time consuming, really improves the taste and
feel of the whole dish. You can prepare both the chickpeas
and the tahini (part of the tarator) in advance, but you'll need
to reheat them over gentle heat and then assemble the dish
just seconds before serving.*

1 Strain the cooked chickpeas, reserving 3 tablespoons of the cooking
liquid.

2 Loosen the chickpea skins by running them under cold water several
times, lastly covering them with water, swish them with your hands
several times to loosen any more skins. Discard any of the loose skins.
Drain the chickpeas again.

3 Mash ⅔ cup of the chickpeas with the reserved liquid to create a
paste. If using canned chickpeas, replace the reserved liquid with water.
Transfer the paste to a bowl, add the warm chickpeas and pour the
tarator over. Mix gently. Drizzle with oil, sprinkle with Aleppo pepper
flakes and sprinkle with parsley. Serve alone or as part of a meze with
warm Arabic Bread.

chargrilled sweet pepper & walnut dip

SERVES 4
PREPARATION TIME: 20 minutes,
* plus roasting the peppers*

1 pound 2 ounces roasted sweet
  pointed peppers (see Roasted
  Vegetables, page 216)

¾ cup walnut halves, roughly
  chopped

⅔ cup fine bread crumbs

2 tablespoons pomegranate
  molasses

½ teaspoon ground cumin

½ teaspoon paprika

¼ teaspoon cayenne pepper

1 teaspoon Aleppo pepper flakes
  (optional)

2 tablespoons olive oil, plus extra
  to drizzle

finely chopped mint leaves,
  to sprinkle

sea salt

warm Arabic Bread (optional, see
  page 217), to serve

Toasted Triangles (optional, see
  page 49)

*The Arabic title of this dip, muhamara, means reddened
or crimsoned. This recipe is traditionally made using sun-
dried Aleppo peppers, finely chopped to a coarse paste. These
peppers, which hail from Syria and neighboring Turkey, have
a high oil content and a hint of earthy smokiness in their
flavor. It isn't easy finding Aleppo pepper paste in the West,
but Aleppo pepper flakes are readily available. Most popular
recipes for this dip involve pureeing, but I prefer it chunky like
this version. It's great as a dip, as well as spread on flatbreads,
mixed into hearty stews or tossed with pasta or potatoes,
in which case you can omit the bread crumbs.*

1 Slice the tops off the roasted peppers, discarding any seeds. Chop the
flesh finely and put it in a mixing bowl.

2 Add the walnuts, bread crumbs, pomegranate molasses, cumin,
paprika, cayenne pepper, Aleppo pepper flakes, if using, and oil and
season to taste with salt. Mix well, then set aside about 1 hour to let the
flavors develop.

3 Put the ingredients in a serving dish, drizzle with olive oil and
sprinkle with mint. Serve at room temperature with warm Arabic Bread.

smoky eggplant dip

SERVES 4
PREPARATION TIME: 10 minutes,
 plus roasting the eggplant

2 ¼ pounds roasted eggplants
 (see Roasted Vegetables, page 216)

2 garlic cloves

5 tablespoons tahini

juice of 1 ½ lemons

olive oil, to drizzle

mint leaves, to sprinkle

seeds from ½ pomegranate
 (see page 216), to sprinkle

sea salt

warm Arabic Bread (see page 217)
 or Toasted Triangles (see page 49),
 to serve

This dish, which you might know as baba ghanouj, is actually known in the Levant as mutabal batinjan (sauced or tossed eggplant). This staple Levantine dip can be found in many variations where beets, zucchini, calamari or pumpkin replace the eggplant (see Shaved Beet, Radish & Grapefruit Salad, page 62). Here, the idea is to add only a trace of tahini so the seductively smoky undertones released by the flames still caress the taste buds.

1 Put the roasted eggplant on a cutting board. Slice off each crown of each eggplant and squeeze out any juices, then transfer the flesh to a mixing bowl. Add the garlic, tahini and half the lemon juice, and season to taste with salt. Toss the mixture together using a fork for a more rustic texture or with a mortar and pestle if you're after a creamier consistency. It's meant to have some body, so don't puree it completely.

2 Taste the dip. If it's too thick, thin it with the remaining lemon juice and adjust the seasoning, as desired.

3 Transfer the mixture to a plate. Create a shallow well in the middle. Drizzle in some oil. Sprinkle the mint leaves and pomegranate seeds over and serve with warm Arabic Bread.

Spinach & Labneh Dip

SERVES 4

PREPARATION TIME: 25 minutes,
 plus chilling and draining the
 yogurt and making the advieh and
 saffron liquid (optional)

COOKING TIME: 15 minutes

2 tablespoons sunflower oil

2 small shallots, finely chopped

1 onion, thinly sliced (optional)

10 ounces spinach leaves

a pinch Advieh 1 (see page 211)

2 garlic cloves, finely chopped

¾ cup plus 2 tablespoons Greek
 yogurt or Labneh Dip (see
 page 221)

a squeeze of lemon juice

1 teaspoon Saffron Liquid (optional,
 see page 212)

sea salt and freshly ground black
 pepper

warm Thin Flatbread (optional, see
 page 218) or Toasted Triangles
 (optional, see page 49), to serve

Booranis are a variety of yogurt-based dishes served as side dishes in Iran. They are cousins of mutabal, where yogurt is used instead of tahini. You can use any kind of green or vegetable instead of the spinach.

1 Heat half the oil in a heavy-bottomed skillet over medium heat. Add the shallots and fry 8 to 10 minutes until soft and lightly golden. Remove the shallots from the pan and set aside. Add the remaining oil to the pan and cook the sliced onion, if using, until golden and crisp. Set aside.

2 Meanwhile, put the spinach in a large saucepan and pour in 4 cups boiling water. Cover and cook over high heat 1 to 2 minutes until it wilts. Rinse the spinach under cold running water, then drain well and squeeze firmly with the back of a spoon to extract as much liquid as you can.

3 Chop the spinach finely and add to the shallots. Add the advieh and garlic and season to taste with salt and pepper. Mix well and return the pan to medium heat. Stir well, cooking 2 minutes longer, then remove the pan from the heat and leave the spinach to cool.

4 Position a colander over a bowl and line the colander with 2 layers of fine cheesecloth. Tip the yogurt in, join the sides of the cloth to create a pouch and close by creating a tight knot. Squeeze the pouch and then leave it to sit in the colander as the whey drains 10 to 15 minutes while the spinach cools. Discard the whey. Alternatively, if you have Labneh Dip on hand (see page 221), you can use that.

5 Once the spinach mixture is cool, transfer it to a serving dish and mix in the strained yogurt. Add a squeeze of lemon juice, then taste and adjust the seasoning, if necessary. Put in the refrigerator 1 hour to chill. Drizzle with saffron liquid and sprinkle with caramelized onion, if using. Serve extremely cold with warm Thin Flatbread.

tabbouleh salad

SERVES 4
PREPARATION TIME: 45 minutes

4 cups flat-leaf parsley leaves (roughly 4 handfuls)

1 tablespoon finely chopped mint leaves

2 cups seeded plum tomatoes cut into ¼-inch cubes

2 small scallions, very finely chopped

2 teaspoons fine bulgur wheat (grade 1), (optional)

crisp romaine lettuce

½ head cabbage

4 fresh grape leaves (optional)

¼ teaspoon ground allspice

juice of 1 lemon

4 tablespoons high-quality extra virgin olive oil

sea salt and freshly ground black pepper

The juice of this salad, known as zoum, is cherished by diners: it's not uncommon to witness children and adults sipping it from their plate. An authentic tabbouleh calls for prolific amounts of parsley, which forms the base of the salad. Bulgur wheat is merely sprinkled over the dish like salt and is not actually an essential ingredient at all. For a real tabbouleh, the most important thing is that the parsley should be cut into very fine threads as carefully as possible, and ideally the blade of the knife should come into contact with it only once. The more the blade is allowed to bruise the parsley, the more bitter it will taste, so a food processor is not a good option. Use the best-quality olive oil you have.

1 Pick out and discard any discolored or imperfect parsley leaves, and discard any stems, which will make the salad bitter. Wash the parsley well, then place in a salad spinner and spin several times until the leaves are completely dry. Alternatively, pat dry thoroughly on paper towels.

2 Bunch up small amounts of the parsley leaves at a time, keeping an extremely tight grip on them, then slice them very thinly (no thicker than 1/16-inch threads) using a very sharp knife. Put into a salad bowl along with the mint, tomatoes and scallions. If preparing for later, cover at this stage and set aside in the refrigerator.

3 Rinse the bulgur, if using, and drain well.

4 Separate the lettuce leaves and the cabbage leaves, and remove their central veins.

5 Arrange the lettuce, cabbage and grape leaves, if using, on a serving plate. When ready to serve, sprinkle the salad with the bulgur wheat, if using. Add the allspice, lemon juice and olive oil and season to taste with salt and pepper. Taste and adjust the seasoning, if necessary. Use the various leaves to scoop up portions of the tabbouleh.

fattoush salad

SERVES 4
PREPARATION TIME: 10 minutes,
  plus making the toasted triangles

juice of 1 ½ lemons

4 tablespoons extra virgin olive oil,
  plus extra for serving

7 ounces mixed green leaves

2 tomatoes, cut into thin wedges

2 small red onions, thinly sliced

1 cup thinly sliced radishes

1 cup cucumbers halved lengthwise
  and thinly sliced

2 tablespoons finely chopped dill
  leaves

a small handful parsley leaves

4 teaspoons sumac

5 tablespoons pomegranate seeds
  (see page 216)

⅔ cup crumbled feta cheese

Toasted Triangles (see page 49)

1 ripe avocado

sea salt and freshly ground black
  pepper

lemon wedges, to serve

Fattoush is a bread salad that has become synonymous with the Middle East. It's a good choice when you want to use up some soon-to-expire vegetables and stale bread. Bread holds a symbolic, almost revered, status in the Middle East. Growing up, I learned if I found a piece on the floor I should pick it up, kiss it and place it somewhere it would be appreciated. "Bread and penny never wasted:" the idea is to make use of what is available and in season. Here is one of the many versions I've made over time.

1 To make the dressing, put most of the lemon juice and the olive oil in a mixing bowl and whisk together. Adjust the sourness by adding more lemon juice, if you want. (Note that the sumac will add a tang to the salad, so it's best to err on the side of caution first and adjust the zing of the salad once it has all been dressed.) Season to taste with salt and pepper. Set aside.

2 Put the mixed leaves, tomatoes, red onions, radishes, cucumber, dill and parsley in a serving bowl and drizzle the dressing over. Toss well, then sprinkle with the sumac, pomegranate seeds, feta and toasted triangles.

3 Cut the avocado in half, remove the pit and scoop out and dice the flesh, then add to the salad and gently toss again. Taste and adjust the seasoning, if necessary. Divide among four bowls and serve with lemon wedges and extra olive oil.

Shaved beet, radish & grapefruit salad

SERVES 4
PREPARATION TIME: 20 minutes

3 tablespoons tahini

1-inch piece gingerroot, peeled and grated

1 garlic clove, finely chopped

5 tablespoons verjuice, or lime juice to taste

3 ounces radishes

14 ounces raw beets, peeled

1 pink grapefruit

1 tablespoon sesame seeds (optional)

2 tablespoons finely chopped dill leaves, plus extra for sprinkling

sea salt and freshly ground black pepper

warm Arabic Bread (see page 217), to serve

This is another dish from the mutabal family (see page 56). Traditionally, beets are boiled for this salad, and then roughly chopped and served with a tarator dressing, but here they are served raw, although if you cannot resist cooking them they can be sautéed for a couple of minutes in sesame oil. I really enjoy the earthiness and crispness of raw beets, and if you want a really spectacular showpiece try combining different colors and varieties. The radishes add a contrast, with their peppery-hot tones, against the sweet-tart grapefruit and the rich, nutty tahini.

1 Put the tahini, ginger and garlic in a bowl and season to taste with salt and slowly pour in the verjuice, whisking quickly as you pour. Set aside. You can prepare this a day ahead to let the flavors develop, if you like.

2 Using a mandolin on the thinnest setting, slice the radishes, then the beets, keeping them separate until assembly. Alternatively, you can use a vegetable peeler or a knife to make very thin slices. Arrange the slices on a large platter or in a shallow serving bowl.

3 Zest the grapefruit using a zester, removing only the colored part of the peel, leaving the bitter white pith. If you don't have a zester, use a vegetable peeler to peel, then finely slice the peel. Put the zest to one side. Peel away and discard any remaining peel and pith and cut the grapefruit into thin slices. Arrange the slices over the beets and radishes.

4 Sprinkle the zest over the salad and pour the tahini dressing over.

5 If using, toast the sesame seeds in a heavy-bottomed pan over medium heat 1 minute, or until golden and fragrant, shaking the pan often. Sprinkle the sesame seeds and dill over the top of the salad and season to taste with pepper. Toss before serving and sprinkle with extra dill. Serve as part of a meze or as a side dish with warm Arabic Bread, if liked.

pomegranate & cucumber salad

SERVES 4
PREPARATION TIME: 20 minutes,
 plus soaking the chickpeas
 (optional)
COOKING TIME: 2 minutes, plus
 cooking the chickpeas until they
 are tender (optional)

1 long cucumber or 4 short Middle
Eastern cucumbers

2 tablespoons pine nuts

seeds from 1 pomegranate (see
page 216)

1 cup dried chickpeas, soaked
overnight and cooked until tender
(see page 215), or 1 can (15-oz.)
chickpeas, drained and rinsed

zest of ½ orange

2 tablespoons finely chopped mint
leaves

2 tablespoons finely snipped chives

3 tablespoons olive oil

2 tablespoons verjuice, or lime juice
to taste

½ cup crumbled feta cheese
or ½ recipe quantity Paneer
Cheese (see page 213), crumbled

sea salt and freshly ground black
pepper

warm Thin Flatbread (see page 218),
to serve

*The simple ingredients in this refreshing salad provide
a contrasting blend of warm, festive colors. It's a beautiful
stand-alone salad and is best served with crusty bread for
a quick lunch or as a side dish to complement a Smoky
Eggplant & Split Pea Stew (see page 168). For nonvegetarians,
choose from a Leafy Lamb Kebab (see page 99) or a plate
of Lamb Rice with Crisp Potato Bottom (see page 109). If using
canned chickpeas is unavoidable, be sure to soak them in
water 10 to 15 minutes and rinse them well under running
water to remove as much of the can flavor as possible.*

1 Peel the cucumber(s), then use a mandolin or a vegetable peeler
to slice them lengthwise into thin ribbons.

2 Toast the pine nuts in a heavy-bottomed pan over medium heat
1 to 2 minutes until golden and fragrant, shaking the pan often.

3 Put the cucumber ribbons, pomegranate seeds, chickpeas, orange
zest, mint, chives and pine nuts in a bowl. Season to taste with salt and
pepper and toss gently.

4 To make the dressing, put the olive oil and verjuice in a small bowl
and whisk to combine.

5 Sprinkle the salad with feta, drizzle with the dressing and serve
immediately with warm Thin Flatbread.

yogurt, cucumber & mint salad

SERVES 4
PREPARATION TIME: 10 minutes

1 cup plus 2 tablespoons Greek yogurt

1 garlic clove

¼ teaspoon sea salt, plus extra for seasoning

1 tablespoon dried mint

1 cup peeled and finely chopped cucumber

freshly ground black pepper

warm Arabic Bread (optional, see page 217), to serve

As refreshing as a cold shower on a blistering-hot day, this salad has the power to improve the character of any dish it accompanies. My favorite use for this salad is as a side dish to kebbeh (see pages 28–9) or Freekeh with Lamb & Rhubarb (see page 110), or atop cold spaghetti. It's equally delicious eaten with warm Arabic bread, as people do in the Middle East.

1 Put the yogurt in a bowl and stir in up to 6 tablespoons water to thin it a bit. The amount needed will depend on the brand of yogurt and the desired consistency of the salad.

2 Crush the garlic with the salt and 2 teaspoons of the mint using a mortar and pestle until it forms a paste. Add the paste to the yogurt and stir well. Add the cucumber and mix well. Taste and adjust the seasoning, if necessary.

3 Cover and set aside in the refrigerator until you are ready to serve. Transfer the salad to a small serving bowl and serve sprinkled with the remaining mint. Enjoy it on its own, as a side dish or spread over warm Arabic Bread, if liked.

undressed herb salad

SERVES 4
PREPARATION TIME: 10 minutes,
  plus making the cheese (optional)

1 handful walnuts (optional)

3 or 4 handfuls any of the following:

mint leaves (all varieties)

basil leaves (all varieties)

tarragon leaves

marjoram leaves

watercress

radishes

cilantro leaves

parsley leaves

scallions

chives

1 recipe quantity Paneer Cheese (see page 213) or 1 heaped cup feta cut into cubes

warm Thin Flatbread (see page 218), to serve

The native name for this dish, sabzi khordan, literally translates as "eating greens," and it's a vital accompaniment to any authentic Persian meal. It's a light and refreshing way to begin any meal, as it awakens the appetite. It's fairly simple to create an undressed salad, just make sure the herbs you use are fresh and in season. A dressing is not usually served, as that would steal the limelight from the real stars of the show.

1 Soak the walnuts, if using, in warm water 5 to 10 minutes until they are soft.

2 Meanwhile, place your selection of herbs and salad vegetables on a serving plate.

3 Drain the walnuts, if using. Add the paneer to the salad, sprinkle with the walnuts and serve with warm Thin Flatbread.

moroccan citrus salad

SERVES 4
PREPARATION TIME: 10 minutes

1 lime

1 orange

1 blood orange

1 pink grapefruit

seeds from 1 pomegranate
  (see page 216)

2 teaspoons roughly chopped
  pistachios

2 tablespoons honey

½ teaspoon orange blossom water
  (optional)

¼ teaspoon ground cinnamon

1 teaspoon chopped mint leaves,
  to sprinkle

TO SERVE (OPTIONAL)
4 tablespoons Greek yogurt

1-inch piece gingerroot, peeled
  and grated

Citrus salads, whether sweet or savory, are very popular in Morocco. As in many parts of the Middle East, most meals end with an array of seasonal fruit: ruby pomegranates, oranges, apples, grapes, loquats, bananas ... It's difficult to provide a recipe for such a basic salad, because it really should come about by following your instinct and mood, so regard this as more of a suggestion than a hard-and-fast recipe: it's now up to you to bring it to life in whatever way you choose. If you want more savory notes, add thin slices of red onion, a creamy cheese, olives, a dash of paprika and a drizzle of argan oil. The combination of fruits and vibrant colors will revive you at first glance, let alone at first bite. Serve with ginger yogurt, if you like.

1 Using a sharp knife, trim the top and bottom of the lime so the flesh is revealed. Keeping the lime upright, cut through the peel downward from top to bottom, following the shape of the fruit, making sure to shave off all the peel and pith. Turn the lime onto its side and cut into thick wheels (not too thick, but thick enough so they are not falling apart). Remove the seeds and arrange the slices on a serving plate so they overlap.

2 Repeat with the remainder of the citrus fruit. Drizzle any juice over the citrus slices.

3 Sprinkle the pomegranate seeds and pistachios over. Put the honey and orange blossom water, if using, in a small mixing bowl and stir well, then drizzle it over the citrus fruits. Dust with cinnamon and sprinkle the mint leaves over.

4 To make the ginger yogurt, if using, put the yogurt and ginger in a bowl and mix well. Serve with the salad.

poultry

Chicken basteeya

SERVES 4
PREPARATION TIME: 30 minutes
COOKING TIME: 1 hour 20 minutes

2 tablespoons sunflower oil

1 onion, finely chopped

1 pound 2 ounces chicken legs
  and thighs

2 garlic cloves, finely chopped

2-inch piece gingerroot, peeled and
  grated

½ teaspoon ground turmeric
  or ground saffron (see page 212)

4 eggs

1 handful cilantro leaves, finely
  chopped

1 handful flat-leaf parsley leaves,
  finely chopped

juice and zest of 1 small lemon

1 cup blanched almonds

3 tablespoons confectioners' sugar,
  plus extra for dusting

⅛ teaspoon ground cinnamon,
  plus extra for dusting

1 tablespoon orange blossom water

7 or 8 sheets phyllo pastry dough,
  depending on the sheet size,
  thawed if frozen

5 tablespoons unsalted butter,
  melted

sea salt and freshly ground black
  pepper

*Traditionally, basteeya is a sweet-and-savory delicacy made
from pigeon layered with crushed almonds and egg, enclosed
in a phyllo-like pastry. I decided to add a literal twist to the
recipe by shaping the basteeya into snakes.*

1 Heat the oil in a deep, heavy-bottomed skillet pan over medium heat.
Add the onion and fry 5 minutes, or until soft and translucent.

2 Season the chicken with salt and pepper and add it to the pan. Sear
3 to 4 minutes, browning on both sides, then drain off any excess fat.
Add the garlic, ginger and turmeric and cook 1 minute, or until aromatic,
tossing the chicken to coat. Cover with 2 cups water and simmer
30 minutes, or until the chicken juices run clear when the thickest part
of a thigh is pierced with the tip of a sharp knife.

3 Remove the chicken from the broth, leaving the broth in the pan,
and set the chicken aside to cool in a bowl. Boil the chicken broth until
it reduces by about half, then whisk in the eggs one at a time until the
eggs and broth form a scramble. You might find you don't need to use
all the eggs. Set aside to cool.

4 Once the chicken is slightly cooler, shred the meat and discard the
bones. Add the herbs and lemon zest and juice to the chicken.

5 Grind the almonds into a rough paste in a food processor, then mix
in the confectioners' sugar, cinnamon and orange blossom water and
stir to combine. Add this to the chicken along with the egg mixture. Stir
to combine. If convenient, you can prepare the recipe to this stage one
day in advance.

6 Heat the oven to 400°F. Remove the sheets of phyllo dough from
their packaging and cover them quickly with a damp dish towel
to stop them drying out. Working with one sheet at a time, evenly
spoon 4 or 5 tablespoons of the chicken mixture along the long edge
of the dough. Roll the dough tightly into a long tube. Repeat with the
remaining phyllo sheets and chicken mixture.

7 Transfer the phyllo rolls to a 12-inch square or round baking pan.
Starting from the outer edge, add the phyllo rolls as you work inward
to cover the bottom of the pan like a coiled snake. Drizzle the melted
butter over the coiled dough and bake 25 to 30 minutes until golden
brown. Lightly dust with cinnamon and confectioners' sugar, then slice
into bite-size pieces. Serve warm.

sumac-scented chicken packages

SERVES 4
PREPARATION TIME: 20 minutes
COOKING TIME: 1 hour

2 skinless chicken legs and 2 skinless
  chicken thighs, weighing about
  1½ pounds in total

½ teaspoon ground allspice

6 tablespoons olive oil

5⅓ cups thinly sliced red onions

2 tablespoons sumac

8 garlic cloves, peeled and crushed
  with the blade of a knife (optional)

4 tablespoons pine nuts

1 cup plus 2 tablespoons dry white
  wine

1 cup plus 2 tablespoons chicken
  stock

4 medium-large loaves bought
  Arabic bread, each about 12 inches
  in diameter, unseparated, or 4
  large soft flour tortillas

sea salt and freshly ground black
  pepper

mixed salad leaves, to serve

*This Palestinian dish called musakhan is traditionally prepared
to celebrate the end of the olive harvest. It's made by slowly
roasting chicken with onions and sumac and then encasing it
in sheets of taboon flatbread that has been lathered in freshly
pressed olive oil. It's perfect for using up leftover chicken or
turkey. Note that the Arabic bread for this recipe has to be
bought, not made to my recipe on page 217, because my
loaves are not large enough for this dish.*

1 Season the chicken with the allspice and salt and pepper. Heat half
the oil in a heavy-bottomed skillet pan over medium heat, then sear the
chicken pieces 5 to 8 minutes on each side. Remove and set aside.

2 Add the rest of the oil to the pan, unless there is still some left, then
add the onions, sumac and garlic, if using. Reduce the heat to low and
cook 10 minutes, or until the onions are soft and slightly caramelized.
Add the pine nuts during the last minutes of the cooking time.

3 Transfer the onion mixture to a plate and deglaze the pan with the
wine, simmering 2 to 3 minutes to reduce it. Pour in the stock and bring
to a boil, then simmer 5 minutes longer, or until the mixture reduces
by about half.

4 Shred the cooked chicken and add it to the skillet pan along with the
onion mixture and mix well to incorporate with the wine broth. Leave to
stand about 5 minutes or so to soak up some of the juices.

5 Meanwhile, heat the oven to 300°F. Place one loaf of bread on the
countertop and spoon one-quarter of the onion mixture with some
of its juices onto the middle of the bread. Create a package by folding
over the edges and wrapping a long piece of kitchen string or sewing
thread around the package lengthwise, keeping the seamless side
down, then twist the string lengthwise to wrap it around the box shape
widthwise. Turn the package over so the seamless side is facing up and
tie the string into a bow on top of the package. Repeat to make the
remaining packages.

6 Place the packages on a baking sheet, seam-side down, and bake
15 to 20 minutes until golden brown and crisp. If you have any
remaining juices in the pan, reserve them for spooning over the opened
packages once they are served.

7 Transfer the cooked packages to four serving plates and remove the
string. Serve with the salad leaves.

slumbering camomile chicken

SERVES 4
PREPARATION TIME: 15 minutes,
  plus brining and resting, and
  making the preserved lemon
COOKING TIME: 1 ¾ hours

3 tablespoons dried camomile (from
  about 10 camomile tea bags)

1 onion, quartered

1 cinnamon stick

3 garlic cloves, crushed with the
  blade of a knife

2-inch piece gingerroot, peeled
  and sliced

¾ cup honey

4 tablespoons coarse sea salt

1 chicken, about 3 pounds 5 ounces

½ cup (1 stick) salted butter,
  softened

3 wedges Preserved Lemon (see
  page 212), peel rinsed and finely
  chopped

4 tablespoons roughly chopped
  tarragon leaves

¾ cup couscous

1 tablespoon all-purpose flour

1 ½ cups broken vermicelli

3 tablespoons sunflower oil

freshly ground black pepper

*This is my version of a Moroccan dish, which produces a juicy
and flavorsome bird. If you don't want to brine the chicken,
add 2 tablespoons honey and camomile to the seasoned
butter in step 4 and adjust to taste with garlic and salt.*

1 If you are brining the chicken, follow steps 1 through 3. Put the
camomile, onion, cinnamon stick, garlic, ginger, ½ cup of the honey
and the salt into a large bowl and add 2 cups plus 2 tablespoons boiling
water. Stir well and leave to cool.

2 Put 2 quarts cold water in a large glass, plastic or other nonmetallic
container, add the cooled brine and mix well. Add the chicken to this
mixture, making sure it is completely covered, then cover and leave
in the refrigerator 4 to 8 hours.

3 About 1 hour prior to cooking, remove the chicken from the brine,
rinse well under cold water and pat dry with paper towels. Strain the
brine and reserve. Place the chicken in a colander over a bowl and leave
to air-dry 30 minutes. Dry the chicken with paper towels.

4 Put 4 tablespoons of the butter, one-third of the preserved lemon and
2 tablespoons of the tarragon in a bowl and mix to create a spreadable
paste. Using your fingers, gently separate the skin from the flesh and dot
the flesh with the butter mixture, spreading it out as much as you can.
Spread a little inside the cavity, too.

5 Place the chicken on a wire rack in a roasting pan and roast about
1½ hours, or until a meat thermometer registers 150°F.

6 Meanwhile, cook the couscous following the directions on page
216, using the reserved brine for steaming, if possible. Don't salt the
couscous until after cooking, and then only if you like. Reserve ½ cup of
the brine.

7 When the chicken is cooked, remove it from the oven and transfer
it to a shallow serving dish, then cover it and set aside. Place the
roasting pan with the juices over two burners on medium heat. Whisk
in the remaining butter and the flour. Add the reserved ½ cup of the
brine, if using, and ½ cup water. Alternatively, add 1 cup water. Whisk
in the remaining honey, the preserved lemon and the tarragon, to form
a thick, pourable sauce.

8 Fry the vermicelli in the oil over medium heat 2 minutes, or until
lightly colored. Toss with the cooked couscous to heat it through,
making sure the mixture is hot. Pour the sauce over the chicken and
sprinkle the couscous-vermicelli mixture over the top. Serve immediately.

Wild thyme chicken

SERVES 4
PREPARATION TIME: 40 minutes,
  plus marinating and resting and
  making the thyme mixture and
  bread
COOKING TIME: 45 minutes

2 garlic cloves, finely chopped

juice of 2 lemons

½ cup olive oil

1 chicken, about 3 pounds 5 ounces

1 tablespoon Wild Thyme Mixture
  (see page 220)

2 loaves warm Arabic Bread (see
  page 217)

2 teaspoons sumac, for dusting

sea salt and freshly ground black
  pepper

TO SERVE
lemon wedges

Garlic Gone Wild (see page 219)

Fattoush Salad (see page 61)
  or Tabbouleh Salad (see page 58)

Swimming Chickpeas (see page 52)
  or Warm Hummus in a Cumin
  & Olive Oil Broth (see page 51)

selection of mixed pickles, such as
  pickled cucumbers, pickled turnips
  and banana peppers

I grew up eating this dish from the Farouj el Lala restaurant, at that time a humble hole in the wall, in Ashrafieh, Beirut. For the best results, cook the chicken on a barbecue using barbecue grill mesh graspers.

1 Put the garlic, lemon juice and olive oil in a small, nonmetallic bowl, mix well and set aside to let the flavors develop.

2 Spatchcock the chicken by placing it breast-side down with the drumsticks facing you. Using a pair of kitchen scissors, cut through the small rib bones around one side of the backbone. Repeat on the other side and then remove the backbone. Turn the chicken over and, using a paring knife, make a small cut in the cartilage in the middle of the top breastbone. Bend the halves backward so the breastbone becomes exposed. Run your paring knife or index fingers down both sides of the breastbone to separate it from the meat, then pull the bone out in one or two pieces. Trim away any excess fat and rinse the chicken. Pat dry.

3 Place the chicken on a baking sheet, season with salt and pepper and pour the lemon and olive oil mixture over the top. Leave to marinate 30 minutes. Meanwhile, depending on your choice, heat a charcoal barbecue until the charcoal is burning white, turn on a gas barbecue to medium–high or heat an oven to 350°F.

4 Press the chicken between the plates of grill mesh graspers, reserving the marinade. The chicken should be sandwiched tightly between the two plates. Place the chicken on the barbecue and cook 5 to 8 minutes on each side.

5 Once the skin develops a slightly pinkish color, baste it with the marinade several times on each side 15 minutes as it cooks. Add the wild thyme mixture and continue 15 to 20 minutes, basting and turning the chicken 3 or 4 more times until the juices run clear when the thickest part of a thigh is pierced with the tip of a sharp knife. Alternatively, put the chicken in a roasting pan and roast in the oven 30 to 45 minutes, basting once or twice and adding the thyme mixture halfway through, then broil the last 5 minutes, if possible, to crisp the skin. Test as above.

6 Peel the Arabic loaves apart at the seam and put half on a serving plate. Lay the whole chicken on top (first releasing it from the graspers, if using), dust with the sumac.

7 Leave to rest 10 minutes, then serve with lemon wedges, Garlic Gone Wild, Fattoush Salad, Swimming Chickpeas, pickles and the remaining bread. Use the bread to help eat the chicken.

sumac chicken casserole

SERVES 4
PREPARATION TIME: 20 minutes
COOKING TIME: 45 minutes

4 chicken legs

1 fennel bulb, quartered

2 potatoes, roughly chopped

1 garlic bulb, crown sliced off and bulb halved

1 onion, quartered

4 tablespoons olive oil

2 tablespoons sumac

½ teaspoon ground allspice

1 bay leaf

1 lemon, for squeezing

sea salt and freshly ground black pepper

Undressed Herb Salad (see page 67) or White Cabbage Salad (see page 220), to serve

This is my brother Eli's take on a popular dish called djej bel furn (chicken in the oven). It exudes simplicity and home comfort and requires only a pinch of time to prepare before everything goes in the oven.

1 Heat the oven to 375°F. Put the chicken legs in a large roasting pan with the fennel, potatoes, garlic and onion. Drizzle the oil over and season with the sumac, allspice, salt and pepper. Add the bay leaf and toss well.

2 Roast 45 minutes, or until the chicken is cooked through: the juices from the chicken should run clear when the thickest part of a thigh is pierced with the tip of a sharp knife. The vegetables should be soft.

3 During the last 10 minutes of the cooking time, change the oven setting to broil or heat a separate broiler and move the pan into it. Broil the chicken pieces 5 minutes, or until the skin is golden and crisp. Squeeze lemon juice to taste over and serve with a salad.

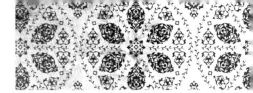

Chicken & Spinach Upside-down Cake

SERVES 4
PREPARATION TIME: 40 minutes
  plus marinating and making the
  advieh, saffron liquid and rice
COOKING TIME: 1 hour 20 minutes

1 cup plus 2 tablespoons Greek yogurt, plus extra to serve

2 egg yolks

1 pound 2 ounces skinless, boneless chicken thighs, cut into ¾-inch cubes

1 tablespoon Advieh 1 (see page 211)

1 large onion, grated

zest of 1 lemon

2 tablespoons sumac

3 garlic cloves, crushed

3 tablespoons Saffron Liquid (see page 212)

1 tablespoon sea salt, plus extra for seasoning

5 tablespoons unsalted butter, diced, plus extra for greasing

1 pound 2 ounces spinach leaves, washed, drained and finely chopped

freshly ground black pepper

1 recipe quantity Parboiled Rice (see pages 214)

Undressed Herb Salad (see page 67), to serve

Here, I have married the classical chicken tahcheen with the spinach version. Tahcheen (arranged at the bottom of the pot) is best cooked in a wide, shallow baking dish and is suitable for preparing in advance. Once turned out onto a serving dish, it makes for a wonderful centerpiece.

1 Put the yogurt and egg yolks in a mixing bowl and beat until well incorporated. Add the chicken, advieh, onion, lemon zest, sumac, garlic, saffron liquid and salt, then season with pepper to taste. Mix well, then cover and leave to marinate in the refrigerator at least 4 hours. At the end of the marinating time, remove the chicken from the refrigerator and bring to room temperature.

2 Heat the oven to 375°F. Generously grease a 2-quart round, clear baking dish with some of the butter and place in the oven to heat 5 minutes, or until the butter is sizzling.

3 Meanwhile, place a skillet over medium-high heat. Add one-quarter of the butter, and the spinach. Cook, tossing often, a few minutes, or until the spinach wilts. Season to taste with salt and pepper. Set aside to cool, then squeeze out as much of the liquid as possible.

4 Using a slotted spoon, remove the chicken from the marinade and set aside. Add half the rice to the marinade and mix well.

5 Once the butter in the oven is sizzling, remove the dish and spread most of the rice and marinade mixture across the base and up the side. Add the chicken and spinach to the rice base and sprinkle with the remaining rice. Gently smooth the surface and sprinkle the remaining pieces of butter across the surface of the rice. Cover tightly with a sheet of lightly buttered foil and bake in the oven 1¼ hours, or until the bottom is golden brown. If you are preparing the dish ahead, put it in the refrigerator once it's covered with foil, then cook it when you're ready.

6 Remove the dish from the oven, uncover and leave to cool 10 minutes. Meanwhile, place a serving plate in the still-warm oven to heat. Serve the rice and tahcheen following the directions in steps 5–7 of Steamed Rice on page 214, with extra yogurt and the Undressed Herb Salad.

Chicken with caraway couscous

SERVES 4
PREPARATION TIME: 15 minutes,
 plus soaking the pearl couscous
 and chickpeas (optional)
COOKING TIME: 45 minutes, plus
 cooking the chickpeas until they
 are tender (optional)

1 cup pearl couscous
 or Italian fregola

4 chicken legs, about 2¼ pounds

1 cinnamon stick

1 bay leaf

1½ teaspoons ground allspice

5 tablespoons salted butter

1½ cups peeled baby pearl onions

1¼ cups dried chickpeas, soaked
 overnight and cooked (see
 page 215), or 2½ cups canned
 chickpeas, drained and rinsed

2 teaspoons caraway seeds

2 tablespoons all-purpose flour

4 tablespoons verjuice, or lime juice
 to taste

sea salt and freshly ground black
 pepper

2 handfuls baby spinach leaves,
 to serve (optional)

Using verjuice (see page 209) and fresh spinach isn't traditional in this dish, which was probably brought to the Middle East by North Africans, but this dish bellows for a bit of greeny goodness. The pearl form of couscous used here is known as moghrabieh.

1 Put the pearl couscous in a heatproof bowl and pour 1 cup 2 tablespoons boiling water over. Stir once and set aside to soak 15 minutes.

2 Put the chicken, cinnamon stick, bay leaf, 1 teaspoon of the allspice and 4⅓ cups water in a large saucepan and heat over medium heat. Season to taste with salt. Place the pearl couscous in a steamer basket or colander set over the pan containing the chicken and broth. Cover and bring to a boil, then reduce the heat to medium-low and simmer 30 minutes until the pearl couscous is tender but not mushy and the chicken is cooked through: the juices from the chicken run clear when the thickest part of a thigh is pierced with the tip of a sharp knife.

3 Meanwhile, heat the oven to 300°F. Melt 2 tablespoons of the butter in a skillet over medium heat. Add the onions and brown them about 5 minutes until they are soft and light golden. Set the pan aside for later use. Transfer the onions to a large ovenproof plate, cover and keep warm in the oven.

4 Once the pearl couscous and chicken are cooked, use a slotted spoon to transfer the chicken to the ovenproof plate, re-cover and return to the oven. Strain and reserve the broth.

5 Add the couscous to the skillet with the chickpeas and onions. Cook 5 minutes, mixing gently so the grains are well coated with the brown butter. Season with the caraway, remaining allspice and salt and pepper to taste. Cover and set aside.

6 Melt the remaining butter in a saucepan over medium-low heat. Add the flour and cook 1 to 2 minutes, stirring constantly, then slowly pour in the verjuice, followed by 2 cups plus 2 tablespoons of the reserved broth a little at a time, whisking vigorously. The mixture will first thicken to a paste before reaching a creamy consistency. Season with salt and pepper, then pour half of the sauce over the pearl couscous, chickpeas and onion mixture, gently mixing to combine well.

7 Heat the broiler to high and broil the chicken 3 to 4 minutes, skin-side up, until lightly golden and crisp. Divide the pearl couscous into bowls and serve with the chicken, remaining sauce and spinach leaves, if you like.

Chicken & preserved lemon tagine

SERVES 4
PREPARATION TIME: 40 minutes,
  plus grinding the saffron and
  making the preserved lemon
COOKING TIME: 50 minutes

1 chicken, about 2¾ pounds

¼ teaspoon ground cinnamon

1 tablespoon sunflower oil

1 large onion, sliced

3 garlic cloves, finely chopped

2-inch piece gingerroot, peeled
  and grated

a pinch ground saffron (see page
  212) or turmeric

2 cups plus 2 tablespoons hot
  chicken stock

1 bay leaf

2 wedges Preserved Lemon (see
  page 212), peel rinsed and
  finely chopped

12 black olives

2 tablespoons finely chopped
  cilantro leaves

sea salt

Couscous (see page 216), to serve

lemon wedges, to serve (optional)

This simple, one-pot tagine dances with flavour. You can steam the couscous over the broth as it cooks (see page 216).

1 Put the chicken breast-side down on a cutting board. Using a small and very sharp knife, cut through the skin between the thigh and the body. Twist the legs gently to remove them from the sockets. Turn the bird back over and ease the legs gently away from the body. Cut through the skin between the thigh and body as far around each leg as possible, keeping the knife as close to the body as you can.

2 Pull the leg away from the body more vigorously and bend it back on itself, so you expose the thigh joint and the ball breaks free of the socket. Cut between the ball and socket to release the leg, and cut through any flesh still attached to the carcass. The "oyster" should still be attached to the thigh.

3 Place a leg, skin-side up, on the cutting board and cut off the knuckle joint at the end of the drumstick. Feel and bend the joint joining the thigh to the drumstick to locate the gap in the bone. Cut through to split the leg into two. Repeat with the other leg and thigh.

4 Next, take a breast and wing off the carcass in one piece. To do this, make a cut through the skin and flesh running along each side of the cartilaginous ridge of the breastbone. Cut the breast meat back, from the cavity end of the chicken down toward and under the wing joint, keeping the knife as close to the carcass as possible. Finish by cutting through the joint where the wing is attached, giving you a breast half with its wing attached. Repeat with the other breast and wing.

5 Lay each of the breast-wing pieces skin-side up on the board and cut slightly on the diagonal into two portions, leaving about one-third of the breast meat attached to the wing. Season with cinnamon and salt.

6 Heat the oil in a heavy-bottomed pan over medium-high heat and brown the chicken pieces, skin-side down. Remove them from the pan and drain on paper towels. Add the onion to the pan, cover and sweat 2 to 3 minutes until translucent, then add the garlic and ginger and cook 1 minute longer, or until the fragrance is released.

7 Stir the saffron into the hot stock and return the chicken to the pan with the onions. Pour over the stock and add the bay leaf, then cover and reduce the heat. Simmer 30 minutes, or until the meat is tender. Add the preserved lemon and olives to the pan and cook 10 minutes longer. Stir in the cilantro and serve with couscous and lemon wedges, if you like.

Jew's mallow with cardamom chicken

SERVES 4
PREPARATION TIME: 30 minutes
COOKING TIME: 1 hour

1 pound 2 ounces chicken breast
  halves, thighs and legs

5 cardamom pods, crushed

1 cinnamon stick

1 bay leaf

1 onion, halved

10 garlic cloves

1 whole nutmeg

2 tablespoons olive oil

2 large shallots, finely chopped

3 handfuls cilantro leaves,
  finely chopped

½ teaspoon ground allspice

2 ¼ pounds fresh or thawed Jew's
  mallow leaves or spinach leaves,
  chopped

½ red onion, finely chopped

⅓ cup apple cider vinegar

2 toasted loaves bought Arabic
  bread, each about 12 inches in
  diameter, crumbled

Vermicelli Rice (see page 215)

salt and freshly ground black pepper

In Arabic, mloukhieh means "of the kings," which refers to the dish, as well as the Jew's mallow leaves that are used. The sweet-scented cardamom, along with the allspice, lends heart-warming flavours to this regal dish. If you can't find fresh Jew's mallow, frozen leaves work just as well, or use spinach instead.

1 Put the chicken, cardamom pods and seeds, cinnamon stick, bay leaf, onion, 1 of the garlic cloves, the nutmeg and 3 ¼ cups water in a deep, heavy-bottomed pan. Season with salt and pepper. Cover and bring to a boil, then reduce the heat to low and leave to simmer about 40 minutes until the chicken is cooked through and the broth is flavorful.

2 Heat the oven to 300°F. Remove the pan from the heat and strain the contents, reserving the broth. Separate the chicken from the spices and aromatics. Transfer the chicken to an ovenproof plate, then shred the meat from the bones or slice it off, cover and keep it warm in the oven.

3 Heat the oil in a deep, heavy-bottomed pan over medium heat. Add the shallots and cook 2 to 3 minutes until soft and translucent. Meanwhile, pound the remaining cloves of garlic into a smooth paste using a mortar and pestle or process in a mini blender. Add the garlic paste to the pan and cook 1 to 2 minutes until fragrant, then add the cilantro and stir well. Pour in the reserved chicken broth, sprinkle in the allspice and stir. Add the chopped Jew's mallow leaves and stir well, then reduce the heat to low and cover partially with a lid. Simmer 10 minutes, checking that the mixture does not come to a boil, otherwise it can coagulate, rendering it inedible. Jew's mallow has natural thickening agents, so don't worry if it looks too runny initially, because it will thicken.

4 Mix the red onion and vinegar in a small bowl and set aside.

5 Dish out the Jew's mallow mixture into a large serving bowl, and place on the table along with the crumbled bread, chicken, onion and vinegar mixture and the Vermicelli Rice, each in its own dish. Diners can then assemble their own dish to their liking, first creating a bed of vermicelli rice, followed by a layer of Jew's mallow with as much juice as they like, then chicken, a sprinkling of crumbled bread and finally a drizzle of the onion and vinegar mixture.

Chicken Stuffed with Cherries

SERVES 4
PREPARATION TIME: 45 minutes,
  plus making the rice and saffron
  liquid
COOKING TIME: 1¾ hours

1⅓ cups dried whole albaloo
  or morello cherries

½ cup dried barberries or
  cranberries

1 tablespoon sunflower oil

1 onion, finely chopped

4 garlic cloves, crushed

⅓ cup whole unsalted pistachios

¼ recipe quantity Parboiled Rice
  (see page 214)

3 tablespoons Saffron Liquid (see
  page 212)

2 tablespoons pomegranate
  molasses

1 teaspoon ground cinnamon

1 chicken, about 1 pound 5 ounces

6 tablespoons unsalted butter

juice of 1 lemon

sea salt and freshly ground black
  pepper

Greek yogurt, to serve

Undressed Herb Salad (see page 67),
  to serve

This dish will turn a traditional Sunday roast into something truly exotic. Trussing the chicken guarantees even cooking, as well as keeping the stuffing in.

1 Heat the oven to 325°F. Soak the dried cherries and barberries in water 5 minutes, then drain and pat dry.

2 Heat the oil in a heavy-bottomed pan over medium heat and fry the onion until soft and translucent. Add the garlic and fry 1 minute longer until fragrant. Add the cherries, barberries, pistachios, rice, 2 tablespoons of the saffron liquid, pomegranate molasses and cinnamon and mix well. Season with salt and pepper to taste. Set aside until completely cool.

3 Rinse the chicken and pat dry, then rub lightly with salt inside and out. Stuff the cavity with the cooled stuffing mixture, then sew up the cavity with a needle and kitchen string.

4 To truss the chicken, place it in front of you on a cutting board, legs facing away from you. Take a 2-foot piece of kitchen string and place the middle point under the tail between the two drumsticks. Pull the two ends of the string up around the dip in the drumsticks, then cross them over and then under each drumstick in a crisscross pattern, pulling the string tight to bring the ends of the drumsticks together. Now, run the string down along the sides of the chicken where the legs and thighs meet and over the inside of the wings. Turn the chicken over, pull gently, and tie the strings tightly under the neck of the bird. Tuck in the wing tips and press down the breast tips if necessary to form a neat package.

5 Put the chicken in a baking dish. Melt the butter in a small, heavy-bottomed saucepan over medium heat, then mix in the lemon juice and remaining saffron liquid. Drizzle the mixture all over the chicken and cover the dish with foil.

6 Roast the chicken about 1½ hours until the juices from the chicken run clear when the thickest part of a thigh is pierced with the tip of a sharp knife. Baste with the juices every 30 minutes.

7 During the last 10 minutes of cooking, remove the foil and change the oven setting to broil (or heat a separate broiler and move the dish into it), then broil on high for a few minutes until the skin is crisp and golden. Remove the string and serve the chicken with yogurt and an Undressed Herb Salad.

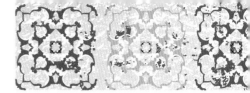

mandaean duck stuffed with nutty ginger rice
with date & apple compote

SERVES 4
PREPARATION TIME: 45 minutes
COOKING TIME: 2¾ hours

¾ cup basmati rice

2-inch piece gingerroot, peeled and thinly sliced

1⅓ cups pitted dried dates, roughly chopped

2¼ cups unsweetened apple juice

2 star anise

1 teaspoon lemon juice

2 tablespoons white wine (optional)

¼ cup blanched almonds

¼ cup pine nuts

¼ cup shelled pistachios

1 duck, about 5½ pounds

½ teaspoon ground cinnamon

½ teaspoon paprika

½ teaspoon ground cardamom

½ teaspoon ground nutmeg

½ teaspoon turmeric

½ teaspoon freshly ground black pepper

½ teaspoon dried lime powder (optional)

sea salt

This recipe is inspired by the spiced duck eaten by the small Mandaean community of Iraq. Traditionally, the duck is boiled and then fried in its own fat. The spices I have used are fairly typical, but the stuffing usually includes golden raisins and onions.

1 Rinse the rice several times in cold water until it runs clear, then drain well. Tip it into a heavy-bottomed saucepan and cover with two times its volume of water. Add the ginger and season with salt, then cover, bring to a rolling boil and boil about 20 minutes.

2 Meanwhile, put the dates, apple juice, star anise, lemon juice and white wine, if using, in a heavy-bottomed saucepan over medium heat and bring to a boil. Reduce the heat to low, then cover the pan and simmer 10 to 15 minutes until the dates are soft and the compote is a thick and sticky sauce. Set aside

3 Meanwhile, toast the almonds in a heavy-bottomed pan 1 minute, then add the pine nuts and pistachios and toast 1 to 2 minutes longer until light brown. Remove the nuts from the pan and roughly chop.

4 Remove the rice from the heat and drain well. Add the nuts and toss to combine.

5 Heat the oven to 325°F. Place the duck on a roasting rack or wire rack set over a roasting pan so the juices drain away and the skin crisps. Lightly prick the skin.

6 Combine all the spices, the black pepper and the dried lime powder, if using, and add salt to taste. Rub the mixture all over the duck inside and out, then stuff the duck with the rice mixture. Sew up the cavity using a needle and strong thread, if you like. It isn't essential, but it does yield the best results.

7 Roast the duck 2 hours, or until the skin is crisp and the meat is tender and falling off the bone, basting it all over with the rendered fat from the bottom of the pan every 20 minutes or so. When ready to serve, carve the duck and serve slices of the meat with the rice and the compote to the side.

duck Shawarma with fig jam

SERVES 4
PREPARATION TIME: 25 minutes,
  plus overnight marinating
COOKING TIME: 2 ¾ hours

4 teaspoons sea salt

½ teaspoon mastic powder
or 4 small mastic tears (see page
209), ground using a mortar
and pestle

½ teaspoon ground mahlab or
ground almonds

1 teaspoon ground cinnamon

1 teaspoon dried mint

1-inch piece gingerroot, grated

8 garlic cloves, finely chopped
or crushed

juice and finely grated zest
of 1 orange

2 cardamom pods, crushed

4 duck legs, skin on

1 teaspoon orange blossom water

1 ¼ cups dried figs

1 tablespoon lemon juice

1 cup sugar

¼ teaspoon fennel seeds or
aniseeds, crushed

4 Thin Flatbreads (see page 218),
to serve

Undressed Herb Salad (see page
67), to serve

*This dish was inspired by a shawarma sandwich I once had at
Ilili restaurant, in New York City. Shawarma is widely believed
to have originated in Anatolia, Turkey, and the name is
derived from the Turkish word "cevirme," meaning "turning,"
referring to the traditional method of cooking it on a spit.*

1 Mix the salt, mastic powder, mahlab, cinnamon, mint, ginger, half
the garlic cloves and the orange zest in a bowl to make a rub. Crush the
cardamom seeds using a mortar and pestle and add to the mixture.

2 Lightly pierce the duck skin all over the legs with the point of a sharp
knife or a skewer, being very careful not to puncture the meat, because
this would make it tough during cooking. Rub the spice mixture over
the legs, then cover and marinate in the refrigerator up to 24 hours.

3 The following day, remove the duck from the refrigerator and bring
it back to room temperature. Heat the oven to 275°F. Put a heavy-
bottomed skillet with a lid and flameproof handle over medium heat.
Add the duck and sear, skin-side down, until the fat is rendered and
the skin is golden and crisp. Flip the duck over so the skin is now facing
upward. Pour in the orange juice and orange blossom water and scrape
up the brown bits from the bottom of the pan. Cover and cook in the
oven 2 ½ hours, or until the flesh just falls off the bones.

4 Meanwhile, put the dried figs in a heavy-bottomed saucepan and
cover with boiling water. Leave to stand 5 minutes, or until the figs
plump up, then remove them with a slotted spoon and reserve the
liquid. Remove the stems from the figs and chop the figs into thin
strands. Return the figs to the pan with the reserved boiling water and
turn the heat to medium.

5 Add the lemon juice, sugar and fennel seeds and stir well. Bring to
a boil, then reduce the heat to low and simmer, stirring often, 15 to
20 minutes until the mixture is thick. To test for doneness, remove a
teaspoon of the mixture and leave it to cool on a plate so you will know
if the jam is set to your liking: slightly runny is best. If the jam is still too
runny, simmer a little longer, then test again.

6 During the last 10 minutes of cooking the duck, change the oven
setting to broil (or heat a separate broiler and move the skillet to it).
Broil the duck for the last 3 to 5 minutes until the skin is crisp and
sizzling. Remove the duck from the oven and use two forks to pull the
tender meat off the bone along with the prized crisp skin. To serve, put
a spoonful of the jam in the middle of each flatbread and top with some
of the duck flesh and crisp skin. Serve with the Undressed Herb Salad.

braised duck legs

SERVES 4
PREPARATION TIME: 30 minutes,
plus roasting the eggplants
COOKING TIME: 1 ¾ hours

4 duck legs, skin on

4 teaspoons finely chopped mint
  leaves, plus extra for sprinkling

sea salt and freshly ground black
  pepper

mint leaves, chopped, to sprinkle

seeds from 1 pomegranate (optional,
  see page 216), to sprinkle

Chelow Rice (see page 214), to serve

FOR THE FESENJÂN CHUTNEY
2 tablespoons sunflower oil

2 shallots, finely chopped

2-inch piece gingerroot, peeled and
  finely chopped

6 garlic cloves, finely chopped

4 tomatoes, finely chopped

½ teaspoon ground cinnamon

1 pound 2 ounces roasted eggplants
  (see Roasted Vegetales, page 216),
  flesh chopped into cubes

½ cup walnut pieces, roughly
  chopped

4 teaspoons pomegranate molasses

sea salt and freshly ground black
  pepper

This is a hearty Iranian stew, traditionally made with game birds and meatballs. Here, I use duck legs instead and make the sauce as a separate chutney. You can serve the chutney with fish and chicken dishes, too.

1 Heat the oven to 325°F. Lightly pierce the duck skin all over the legs with the point of a sharp knife or a skewer, being very careful not to puncture the meat, because this will make it toughen during cooking. Season with salt and pepper.

2 Put a large, dry skillet pan that can hold the duck legs in a single layer over medium heat. Add the duck legs to the pan, skin-side down, and sear 5 to 10 minutes until the skin is crisp and much of the fat is rendered.

3 Transfer the duck legs to a wire rack with a roasting pan underneath to collect the fat, and roast in the middle of the oven about 1 ½ hours until the meat is cooked through and tender and the skin is crisp and brown. Meanwhile, leave the skillet to cool. If you want the skin to be more crisp, during the last 10 minutes of cooking, change the oven setting to broil (or heat a separate broiler and move the pan under it), then broil on high the last 2 to 3 minutes.

4 Meanwhile, pour 1 ¼ cups boiling water over the cooled duck fat in the skillet. Stir the mixture, which will have all the rich flavors of the duck, then set aside.

5 About 15 minutes before the duck should finish cooking, make the fesenjân chutney. Heat the oil in a heavy-bottomed saucepan over medium heat. Add the shallots and ginger, then cover and sweat 2 to 3 minutes. Add the garlic, tomatoes and cinnamon and cook about 1 minute until fragrant, then pour the reserved duck water from step 4 over. Bring the mixture to a boil, then reduce the heat to low, add the chopped eggplant and walnuts and mix well. Simmer about 5 minutes, then season to taste with salt and pepper.

6 Remove the pan from the heat and stir in the pomegranate molasses. Adjust the seasoning to taste, if needed. Sprinkle the duck legs with mint and pomegranate seeds, if using, and serve with the chutney and Chelow Rice.

Note: If you are in a rush or preparing this dish for a large number of guests, you can skip the searing step and simply broil the duck at the end to help crisp the skin. Use a flavorsome stock with the chutney in place of the duck fat water from step 4.

meat

chickpea flour quiche

SERVES 4
PREPARATION TIME: 10 minutes,
 plus resting and making the
 harissa
COOKING TIME: 25 minutes

butter, for greasing

2 tablespoons olive oil

5 ounces boneless lamb shoulder, fat
 removed and the flesh sliced into
 thin slivers

2 cups chickpea flour or gram flour

1 ½ teaspoons cumin, plus extra
 for sprinkling

½ teaspoon sea salt, plus extra
 for seasoning

3 ¼ cups milk

2 eggs

¼ teaspoon Harissa (see page 210)

3 ounces sun-blushed tomatoes

Undressed Herb Salad (see page 67),
 to serve

Cumin, lamb and chickpeas are a celestial combination, and no more so than in this North African quichelike dish, sold along the streets of eastern Morocco and western Algeria by the slice, sandwiched in a baguette. Traditionally, it's a simple combination of gram flour (chickpea flour), milk or water, eggs and a sprinkling of cumin. It's incredibly versatile and lends itself well to so many flavors, such as caramelized onions, goat cheese, shredded artichokes, spinach, bacon, olives…you can really go wild with this. It's meant to be served slightly wet and wobbly, although some people prefer it drier and more cooked. It's gluten free, and water can be substituted for milk.

1 Heat the oven to 350°F and lightly grease a 9-inch quiche dish or other round baking dish with butter.

2 Heat half the oil in a skillet over medium heat. Add the lamb and sear about 2 minutes until cooked through, stirring often.

3 Put the chickpea flour, cumin, salt, milk, eggs, harissa and remaining oil in a mixing bowl and pulse with a stick blender until you achieve a smooth, frothy, liquid mixture with an airy texture. Add a little salt, but not too much because the sun-blushed tomatoes you will be adding are already salted.

4 Add the cooked lamb, discarding the oil and juices released after cooking, and stir to combine, then pour the mixture into the greased dish and scatter the sun-blushed tomatoes over.

5 Bake the quiche in the oven 20 minutes. During the last 5 minutes of baking, change the oven setting to broiler (or heat a separate broiler and move the dish into it), then broil the quiche on high the last few minutes to brown the top. Remove the quiche from the oven and leave the quiche to rest a few minutes before slicing. Serve warm, sprinkled with more cumin, if you like, and with the Undressed Herb Salad on the side.

eggplant-wrapped fingers

SERVES 4
PREPARATION TIME: 30 minutes,
  plus resting
COOKING TIME: 1 hour 10 minutes

2 eggplants

5 tablespoons olive oil

9 ounces ground lamb or veal

1 onion, finely chopped

1 tablespoon pomegranate molasses

1 tablespoon finely chopped
  cilantro leaves

¼ teaspoon ground cardamom

¼ teaspoon ground allspice

a pinch dried chili flakes (optional)

2¼ cups tomato puree

3 garlic cloves, finely chopped
  or crushed

2 tablespoons pine nuts

sea salt and freshly ground black
  pepper

Greek yogurt, to serve

chopped mint leaves, to sprinkle

Arabic bread (see page 217), to
  serve

These are the Middle Eastern version of involtinis. Known as lisan el qadi in Arabic, they literally translate as "tongue of the judge." Long, thin slices of eggplant are rolled to wrap the meat. Their name was possibly inspired by the fact that Iraqis are so fond of meat that a noble judge would always expect his food to be served with meat rather than rice.

1 Heat the oven to 350°F. Slice the eggplants lengthwise into ⅛-inch-thick slices; you should get about 16 slices. Brush each slice with oil on both sides, then put them in a baking dish (one you can reuse later to finish cooking the eggplant rolls in the sauce) and bake 20 minutes, turning them once halfway, until they are cooked through and golden but not charred. You might need to cook them in batches. Transfer the slices to a plate lined with paper towels and leave to one side until cool enough to handle.

2 Meanwhile, add the ground meat to a bowl with the onion, pomegranate molasses, cilantro, cardamom, allspice and chili flakes, if using. Season to taste with salt and pepper. Mix well to incorporate, then divide the meat into sausage-shaped portions or "fingers," 1 inch thick and 2 inches long.

3 When the eggplant slices are cool, lay one of them on the countertop, with the wider end facing you. Place a meat finger at the end of the eggplant slice and begin rolling it up tightly. Continue with the remaining eggplant slices and meat fingers. Transfer the rolls to the dish, seam-side down and making sure they fit snugly. Put the tomato puree and garlic in a bowl and season to taste with salt and pepper. Pour the tomato puree sauce over the eggplant rolls, then cover the dish with foil and bake in the oven 45 minutes.

4 Remove the dish from the oven and leave the eggplant rolls to rest at least 10 minutes. Meanwhile, toast the pine nuts in a heavy-bottomed pan over medium heat 1 to 2 minutes until golden and fragrant, shaking the pan often.

5 Put the meat fingers on a bed of yogurt, with the sauce poured over and sprinkled with the toasted pine nuts and mint. Serve with Arabic bread.

Leafy Lamb Kebabs

SERVES 4
PREPARATION TIME: 20 minutes,
 plus marinating
COOKING TIME: 5 minutes

¼ cup sunflower oil, plus extra
 for oiling

¼ cup verjuice, or lime juice to taste

1 heaped tablespoon sumac

1 pound 2 ounces lamb tenderloin

2 onions, thinly sliced

12 cherry tomatoes

sea salt and freshly ground black
 pepper

Chelow Rice (see page 214), to serve

warm Thin Flatbread (see page
 218), to serve

The original name for this dish is kabâb-e barg. Barg translates as "leaf," and you need to cut your meat into long, thin strips. If tenderloin is hard to find, you can use two neck fillets instead. Lime juice can be substituted for the sweet tang of verjuice. The more fat or oil there is in the marinade, the more tender the results will be. For the best results, marinate the lamb overnight and use wide skewers.

1 To make the marinade, put the oil, verjuice and sumac in a nonmetallic bowl and mix well until the ingredients emulsify.

2 With a sharp knife, divide the lamb into 4–6 equal portions about 2½ inches long. Working with one portion at a time, flatten each portion slightly with the palm of your hand, then cut through at about ½ inch from the top, horizontally, making sure not to sever the flesh completely. Open it out to form one longer slice, and then repeat the same process in the other direction from the bottom so that you end up with one long leafy strip. Each strip should ideally be about 7 inches long and less than ½ inch thick. Trim the edges so the strip has straight lines, then use a meat mallet to soften and stretch the meat.

3 Carefully weave a wooden skewer through each strip of meat. Put 2 to 3 kebabs in a shallow dish and sprinkle with a little onion and half the marinade. Repeat with the remaining kebabs, onion and marinade.

4 Leave the kebabs to marinate in the refrigerator at least 8 hours or overnight, turning the kebabs in the marinade a couple of times during this period. Just before putting the lamb on the barbecue, shake off most of the marinade and season to taste with salt and pepper. Reserve the onions for grilling.

5 Heat a charcoal barbecue until the charcoal is burning white or heat a gas barbecue to high. Oil the grill rack. Grill the kebabs just 1 to 2 minutes on each side. You can also barbecue the tomatoes and onions at the same time, using a vegetable basket, until golden and caramelized. Alternatively, cook them in a griddle pan.

6 Serve the kebabs immediately with the caramelized onions, the barbecued tomatoes and with Chelow Rice and warm Thin Flatbread.

caramelized onions stuffed with lamb

SERVES 4
PREPARATION TIME: 35 minutes
COOKING TIME: 1½ hours

9 ounces ground lamb

¼ cup short-grain white rice or risotto rice

½ teaspoon ground allspice

½ teaspoon ground cinnamon

2 teaspoons dried mint

1 tablespoon tomato paste

1 tablespoon pine nuts (optional)

about 1 tablespoon sea salt, plus extra for seasoning

4 or 5 large white onions

1 tablespoon tamarind paste

juice of 1 lemon

freshly ground black pepper

Greek yogurt, to serve

green salad of your choice, to serve

This dish is dedicated to Aunty Suham, the mother of my dear friends Dhabia and Wid, who first introduced me to these moreish dolmas at an unforgettable feast she prepared when I asked her about some Iraqi dishes for this cookbook. Many of the dishes she made that evening have made it into this book, and I'm forever grateful to her. It's important to use large onions because the layers have more surface area, making them more suited for stuffing and rolling. The number of onions required will vary depending on how many layers you can get out of each onion. If you like them more meltingly soft, you can cook them for a little longer. The dolmas are easy to make, but you do need to make sure the onions are blanched enough to be very pliable. The stuffed onions are usually cooked with other dolmas, such as Grape Leaves with Bulgur, Figs & Nuts (see page 160), but never cabbage leaves, because they're too similar in appearance to onions, potentially confusing diners.

1 Put the lamb, rice, spices, mint and tomato paste in a mixing bowl and season with salt and pepper.

2 Toast the pine nuts, if using, in a heavy-bottomed pan over medium heat 1 to 2 minutes until golden and fragrant, shaking the pan often. Add the toasted pine nuts to the lamb mixture and mix well to incorporate.

3 Half-fill a large saucepan with water, sprinkle in the salt and bring to a boil over high heat. Meanwhile, slice off the tops and bottoms of the onions. Without cutting right through them, cut the onion in half lengthwise, stopping about halfway through each one. Remove the skins, then gently remove the root strands and any shorter layers that will be too short for stuffing and rolling. Set these aside for use in the stuffing later. You should have 5 or 6 outer layers per onion to work with.

4 Once the water boils, add the onion layers that are large enough for stuffing, then reduce the heat to low, cover with a lid and simmer 10 minutes, or until the onion layers begin to soften and come apart. You want them to be pliable enough so they are easy to roll. Remove the

herbed kafta with dukkah tahini

SERVES 4
PREPARATION TIME: 45 minutes
COOKING TIME: 50 minutes

1 large onion, quartered

2 handfuls mixed herb leaves (mint, dill, cilantro and parsley)

2 mild red chilies, seeded and roughly chopped (optional)

6 garlic cloves, crushed with the blade of a knife

1 pound 2 ounces ground lamb

1 ½ teaspoons ground allspice

½ teaspoon coriander seeds

½ teaspoon cumin seeds

1 teaspoon sesame seeds

½ teaspoon dried mint

½ teaspoon poppy seeds (optional)

⅔ cup tahini

5 tablespoons lemon juice

1 tablespoon olive oil

sea salt

Potato Matchsticks (see page 218), to serve

mixed salad, to serve

Known as kafta b tahini, this dish is particularly popular in Palestine. While not traditional, I've added to the tahini an Egyptian mix of spices, herbs and seeds, known as dukkah, which also traditionally includes nuts.

1 Put the onion in a food processor and pulse to form a rough paste. Squeeze out as much of the liquid as possible. Return the mixture to the food processor, add the herbs, chilies and garlic and pulse again 1 to 2 minutes until the mixture forms a fine paste.

2 Put the lamb in a large mixing bowl. Add the allspice, season to taste with salt and knead the herb and onion mixture with the meat 1 to 2 minutes until well incorporated. Don't overwork it or the meat will toughen. Cover and set aside.

3 Meanwhile, prepare the dukkah mixture by toasting the coriander and cumin seeds in a heavy-bottomed pan over medium heat 1 to 2 minutes until fragrant, shaking the pan often. Transfer to a small food processor or spice grinder and grind to a rough consistency.

4 Return the spice mixture to the pan, add the sesame seeds and continue to cook until golden, then remove the pan from the heat. Add the dried mint, poppy seeds, if using, and season to taste with salt. Set aside.

5 Put the tahini in a mixing bowl and slowly stir in as much of ⅔ cup water as is needed to reach a creamy consistency. Also add a little of the lemon juice as you go until the tahini is creamy consistency and as sharp as you like it. Make sure the mixture is runny (it will thicken with cooking), by adding more lemon juice or water to taste. You might not need all the lemon juice. Sprinkle in the dukkah mixture and stir well.

6 Heat the oven to 400°F. Meanwhile, mold the meat mixture into 16 patties, about 2 inches in diameter. Heat 1 tablespoon of the oil in a large skillet with an ovenproof handle over medium heat. Add the patties and cook about 2 minutes on each side until brown, then remove the pan from the heat.

7 Pour the tahini mixture over the patties, cover the pan with the lid or foil and bake 45 minutes.

8 Once the kafta have finished cooking, test the tahini mixture around the patties: it will have dried a bit and the tahini will hug the patties snuggly. If you want to have more of a sauce, thin it with a little water before serving with Potato Matchsticks and a mixed salad.

spiced lamb flatbread pizzas

SERVES 4
PREPARATION TIME: 25 minutes,
 plus making the dough
COOKING TIME: 5 to 7 minutes

2 large onions, very finely chopped

4 large plum tomatoes, very finely
 chopped

1 teaspoon sea salt

14 ounces finely ground lamb

1 teaspoon ground cinnamon

1 teaspoon ground allspice

1 teaspoon hot chili flakes

2 tablespoons pomegranate
 molasses

1 recipe quantity Arabic Bread
 dough (see page 217)

all-purpose flour, for dusting

3 tablespoons pine nuts

TO SERVE
Undressed Herb Salad (see page 67)

Harissa (see page 210)

Savory Yogurt Shake (see page 221)

lemon halves

*Although these are known by Armenians as missahatz,
by Turks as lahmacun and by the Lebanese as lahm b'ajeen,
the basic idea is the same: meat spread on bread. The best
flatbread pizzas I've ever had, second to this recipe, of course,
was at an Armenian bakery called Furn Ikhshanian, in Zokak
el Blat, a district of Beirut. The reason they were so good was
their paper-thin and crisp crust. Flatbread pizzas belong
to the manaquiche family, and while manaquiche are
considered a breakfast food, they are also enjoyed throughout
the day, and there is a predominant after-club culture
of tucking into these after a heavy night out! They're best
when washed down with a savory yogurt shake.*

1 Put the onions and tomatoes in a bowl. Note that they must be
chopped almost to a paste. Sprinkle the paste with the salt and set aside
5 minutes, then squeeze out as much liquid as possible.

2 Put the well-squeezed tomatoes and onions in a bowl with the lamb,
sprinkle with the cinnamon, allspice and chili flakes and drizzle with the
pomegranate molasses, then mix well.

3 Heat the oven to 500°F. Divide the bread dough into 4 equal-size
balls and dust the work surface with flour. Roll out each ball into
a 12-inch circle (the dough should be paper thin). Using your fingers,
gently spread one-quarter of the meat mixture over each pizza evenly
and thinly. Sprinkle the pine nuts over the pizzas.

4 Transfer the pizzas onto perforated, round pizza crispers and bake
in the oven 5 to 7 minutes until the edges of the pizzas are golden
brown and crisp. Alternatively, use cookie sheets to slide the pizzas
straight onto the oven shelves. Serve with Undressed Herb Salad,
Harissa and Savory Yogurt Shake, with lemon halves for squeezing.

lamb rice with crisp potato base

SERVES 4
PREPARATION TIME: 30 minutes,
* plus making the advieh and rice*
COOKING TIME: 1 ½ hours

½ cup sunflower oil

1 onion, finely chopped, plus
  1 onion, thinly sliced

4 garlic cloves, finely chopped

1 pound 2 ounces boneless lamb
  (preferably leg), fat trimmed off
  and the flesh cut into ½-inch cubes

2 teaspoons Advieh 1 (see page 211)

a pinch ground cinnamon

5 tablespoons tomato paste

3½ cups seeded large tomatoes cut
  into ½-inch cubes

1 pound 2 ounces salad potatoes,
  peeled, half cut into ½-inch cubes,
  the other half sliced lengthwise into
  long, thin ovals about ⅛ inch thick

1 recipe quantity Parboiled Rice (see
  pages 214)

chopped mint leaves, to sprinkle

sea salt and freshly ground black
  pepper

Greek yogurt or kashk, to serve

This is my take on a layered rice recipe known as Istambooli Polow. At first glance it does sound like a carb-on-carb sin, with its combination of potato and rice, but don't judge it until you have tried it. Turkey also works well instead of lamb.

1 Heat 2 tablespoons of the oil in a skillet over medium-low heat. Add the chopped onion and sauté 4 to 5 minutes until soft and translucent. Add the garlic, lamb, spices, tomato paste and tomatoes, and season to taste with salt and pepper. Add ½ cup water less 2 tablespoons, or enough to cover the other ingredients, then increase the heat to high and bring to a boil. Reduce the heat to low and leave to simmer 1 hour, or until the meat is tender and the sauce is thick. Remove the pan from the heat and stir in the potato cubes.

2 Place a 8¾-cup nonstick saucepan with an 8-inch base over medium heat and pour in 5 tablespoons of the oil. Once the oil is sizzling, arrange the potato slices across the bottom (they can overlap slightly), then sprinkle 2 tablespoons of the lamb and tomato mixture over, followed by a layer of rice. Continue alternating layers of lamb and rice, building it up into a dome shape. The last layer should be rice.

3 Using the handle of a wooden spoon, make three holes in the rice all the way to the bottom, being careful not to puncture the potatoes.

4 Wrap the saucepan lid in a clean dish towel and tie it into a tight knot at the handle, then use it to cover the pan as tightly as you can so that steam doesn't escape. (The dish towel prevents the moisture dripping onto the rice, making it soggy.) Cook the rice over medium heat 2 to 3 minutes until the rice is steaming (you will see puffs of steam escaping at the edges of the lid), then reduce the heat to low and cook 20 to 25 minutes, with the lid on all the time.

5 Meanwhile, heat the remaining oil in a skillet over medium-low heat, and fry the sliced onion until crisp and golden.

6 Serve the rice and tahdeeg following the directions in steps 5–7 of Steamed Rice on page 214. Sprinkle with mint and serve with yogurt and the fried onion rings.

freekeh with lamb & rhubarb

SERVES 4
PREPARATION TIME: 25 minutes,
 plus making the stock
COOKING TIME: 2 hours

2 tablespoons salted butter

8 ounces pearl onions or small
 shallots, peeled

2 pounds lamb shank(s)

½ teaspoon ground allspice

2 teaspoons Aleppo pepper flakes
 or crushed chili flakes

2-inch piece gingerroot, peeled and
 chopped very finely

6 garlic cloves, crushed with the
 blade of a knife

1 bay leaf

¼ teaspoon coriander seeds

2½ quarts Vegetable Stock (see
 page 211)

2½ cups wholegrain freekeh or
 farro, rinsed well

2 cups rhubarb cut into 1-inch pieces

2 tablespoons pine nuts

¼ cup blanched almonds

2 tablespoons roughly chopped
 cilantro leaves, to sprinkle

sea salt and freshly ground black
 pepper

Greek yogurt, to serve

Freekeh is my number one grain. The wheat is harvested young, when the grains are soft and full of moisture. The grain is then sun-dried before being roasted over an open fire several minutes. Once cool, it's rubbed to separate it from the chaff. It can be purchased cracked or whole, and will often require careful cleaning to rid it of any stones.

1 Melt 4 teaspoons of the butter in a large heavy-bottomed saucepan over medium-low heat and fry the pearl onions 3 to 4 minutes until golden. Remove the onions from the pan and set aside.

2 Rub the lamb shank(s) all over with the allspice and Aleppo pepper flakes and season to taste with salt and pepper, then transfer to the saucepan.

3 Return the onions to the pan, and sear the onions and lamb until brown all over. Remove the shank and set aside on a plate.

4 Add half the remaining butter to the pan, along with the ginger, garlic, bay leaf and coriander seeds and cook 1 minute, or until aromatic. Return the lamb shank and pour 4⅓ cups of the stock over, then cover the pan with a lid, reduce the heat to low and simmer 1¾ hours, turning the shank around a couple of times while cooking.

5 Meanwhile, put the freekeh in a saucepan and pour the remaining stock over, then cover the pan and bring to a boil. Reduce the heat to low and leave to simmer about 45 minutes until the stock is absorbed and the grains are cooked through but still have a slight bite to them. If the grains are not cooked through, in this time, but the stock is all absorbed, add a little water as needed. Once cooked, set aside, covered, until ready to serve.

6 Just before the lamb stew finishes cooking, melt the remaining butter in a pan over medium heat, add the rhubarb and toss to combine, then cook 4 minutes, or until just beginning to soften.

7 Spoon the rhubarb into the lamb stew and toss well, then remove the stew from the heat and leave it to sit, covered, 5 minutes.

8 Toast the pine nuts and almonds in a heavy-bottomed pan over medium heat 1 to 2 minutes until golden and fragrant, shaking the pan often.

9 Transfer the freekeh to a serving plate and top with the lamb stew and rhubarb. Sprinkle with the nuts and cilantro and serve with yogurt.

auntie anwaar's mansaf risotto

SERVES 4
PREPARATION TIME: 15 minutes,
  plus making the bread
COOKING TIME: 1 ½ hours

2 tablespoons salted butter

1 pound 14 ounces lamb shank(s)

2 carrots, roughly chopped

1 onion, quartered

10 garlic cloves, 5 left whole and
  5 pounded using a mortar and
  pestle or crushed

6 cardamom pods

1 bay leaf

1 cinnamon stick

1 cup short-grain or risotto rice

1 teaspoon turmeric

3 ¼ cups Greek yogurt

1 egg

1 tablespoon cornstarch, if needed

3 tablespoons pine nuts

3 tablespoons blanched almonds

juice of 2 lemons

2 loaves warm Arabic Bread (see
  page 217)

mint leaves, finely chopped,
  to sprinkle

sea salt and freshly ground black
  pepper

Traditionally, this quintessentially Bedouin dish is prepared using jmeed, which is a dried yogurt or buttermilk sometimes called rock cheese. Anwaar Younis gave me her recipe for Jordan's national dish, which I've tweaked a little. Mansaf is a communal dish and a great symbol of generosity that is often served on special occasions. Sometimes eaten with the right hand, the meat is torn apart and rolled into a ball, which is then dipped into the yogurt. Jmeed is not easy to source in the West, so I have suggested Greek yogurt instead.

1 Melt the butter in a heavy-bottomed saucepan over medium heat. Add the lamb shank(s), carrots, onion, whole garlic cloves, cardamom pods, bay leaf and cinnamon stick and cook 4 to 5 minutes, turning frequently, until the meat is brown. Season with salt to taste, then cover with 5 cups water and bring to a boil. Reduce the heat to low, then cover and simmer 1 hour, or until the meat is tender and falling off the bone(s). Strain well, reserving the stock and the meat, but discarding the vegetables and spices.

2 Put the rice, 3 ¼ cups of the reserved stock and the turmeric in a separate heavy-bottomed pan over medium heat. Bring to a boil, then reduce the heat to low and simmer 25 minutes, or until the rice is cooked through and all the stock is absorbed, adding a little more stock as needed and stirring every so often to achieve a creamy texture. Season to taste with salt and pepper.

3 Meanwhile, separate the meat from the bone and cut into small pieces. Put the yogurt in the pan the meat was cooked in and place over medium heat, then add the egg and whisk well. Return the meat to the pan and bring the mixture to a gentle boil. Reduce the heat to low and simmer, stirring often so that the yogurt doesn't catch, for 15 to 20 minutes until the yogurt is thick and creamy. If the mixture is too runny, add the cornflour and mix until thickened.

4 Toast the pine nuts and almonds in a heavy-bottomed pan over medium heat 1 to 2 minutes until golden, shaking the pan often.

5 Put the crushed garlic in a small bowl, add the lemon juice and mix. To serve, lay the Arabic Bread on a large serving platter and pour the garlic mixture over it. Spoon the rice over, then spoon a couple of tablespoons of the cooked yogurt over. Scatter with the meat pieces and then sprinkle the toasted nuts and mint over. Serve the remaining cooked yogurt on the side.

meaty ratatouille

SERVES 4
PREPARATION TIME: 25 minutes
COOKING TIME: 30 minutes

3 tablespoons olive oil

3 onions, thinly sliced

1 garlic bulb, cloves separated and crushed with the blade of a knife

9 ounces ground lamb, beef or pork

¼ teaspoon ground cinnamon

½ teaspoon ground allspice

1 large zucchini, roughly chopped

2 carrots, roughly chopped

1 large potato, roughly chopped

7 small tomatoes, quartered

2 thyme sprigs (optional)

2 heaped tablespoons tomato paste

1 eggplant, roughly chopped

2 tablespoons pine nuts, to sprinkle

sea salt

Vermicelli Rice (see page 215), to serve

Greek yogurt, to serve (optional)

Think of this as a Lebanese relative of ratatouille, if you like. It's about using fresh produce from the garden or market, as available, and layering them in a pot. You can make it as chunky or as fine as you like. Just make sure the eggplant is cut into the largest pieces you can, because they cook the fastest. The kind of tomatoes you use here are important so do taste and adjust, adding more or less tomato paste for color and richness when needed.

1 Heat the oil in a large, heavy-bottomed saucepan over medium heat. Add the onions and garlic and let them sweat 3 to 5 minutes until soft and translucent.

2 Add the ground lamb, cinnamon and allspice and season with salt. Stir well, then cook 2 to 3 minutes longer until brown.

3 Add the zucchini, carrots, potato, tomatoes and thyme, if using. Dilute the tomato paste in about 3 cups water and pour into the pan and stir well. Cover and bring to a boil, then reduce the heat to low. Add the eggplant and simmer 20 minutes, or until the vegetables are cooked but still have a slight bite to them.

4 Meanwhile, toast the pine nuts in a heavy-bottomed pan over medium heat 1 to 2 minutes until golden and fragrant, shaking the pan often.

5 Sprinkle the toasted pine nuts over the ratatouille and serve with Vermicelli Rice and yogurt, if you like.

lamb & herb stew

SERVES 4
PREPARATION TIME: 30 minutes
  plus overnight soaking
COOKING TIME: 2 to 2½ hours

heaped ½ cup dried red kidney
  beans, soaked overnight

2 tablespoons sunflower oil

1 onion, finely chopped

1 leek, finely chopped

1 handful chives, finely snipped

1 handful fenugreek leaves
  or 1 tablespoon dried fenugreek

1 handful finely chopped dill leaves,
  plus extra for sprinkling

2 handfuls parsley leaves

2 handfuls cilantro leaves

14 ounces boneless lamb shoulder,
  cut into ¾-inch cubes

4 whole dried black limes (limu
  amani), pierced with the tip
  of a knife (optional)

juice of 2 lemons

sea salt and freshly ground black
  pepper

Chelow Rice (see page 214), to serve

Greek yogurt, to serve

Upon first sight, you might not be compelled to try one of Iran's most popular dishes, known locally as ghormeh-e sabzi. But don't be misled by first impressions. This dish is a splendid testimony to the Persian love of herbs and fragrance, and is a harmonious melange of texture and flavor. For an equally fulfilling vegetarian option, double the kidney bean portion to make up for the absent lamb.

1 Put the red kidney beans in a deep, heavy-bottomed saucepan and cover with water. Bring to a rolling boil over high heat, then continue to boil 10 to 15 minutes until the beans are tender but with a slight bite to them. Drain and set aside.

2 Meanwhile, heat the oil in a heavy-bottomed saucepan or Dutch oven over medium heat. Add the onion and leek and fry 5 minutes until soft and golden.

3 Add all the herbs and stir well, then cook 10 minutes until fragrant, stirring often. Increase the heat to high, add the lamb and stir well to coat with the onion and leeks, then cook about 2 minutes until the meat is brown on all sides.

4 Add the drained kidney beans to the pan, cover with water and bring to a boil. Reduce the heat to low, then cover with a lid and simmer 1½ to 2 hours until the beans are soft, the meat is tender and the sauce reduced and well blended.

5 When the stew has been simmering for about an hour, add the dried limes, if using (any sooner and they will turn the stew bitter), pushing them down into the liquid. They will tend to pop back up, so try to cover them with a few pieces of meat to keep them submerged.

6 Just before serving, season the dish with lemon juice and salt and pepper to taste and mix well. Serve with the Chelow Rice and yogurt.

baked spiced lamb tortellini

SERVES 4
PREPARATION TIME: 1 hour,
  plus resting and making the herb
  butter
COOKING TIME: 25 minutes

⅔ cup flour, plus extra to dust

⅔ cup semolina flour, plus extra
  to dust

1 teaspoon sea salt, plus extra
  for seasoning

3 eggs

½ teaspoon extra virgin olive oil

2 tablespoons sunflower oil

1 onion, finely chopped

9 ounces finely ground lamb or beef

½ teaspoon ground cinnamon

½ teaspoon ground allspice

½ teaspoon dried chili flakes

3 cups Greek yogurt

1 tablespoon cornstarch, if needed

⅓ cup pine nuts

Herb Butter (see page 211), to serve

sumac, to sprinkle

Vermicelli Rice (see page 215),
  to serve (optional)

Known as shish barak in Lebanon, Syria and Palestine, the Armenians and Turks have a variation called manti. I love making them with friends while sharing a bottle of wine.

1 Sift together both flours and the salt onto the countertop. Create a well in the middle, add 2 of the eggs and the olive oil and mix gently with a fork, gradually incorporating the eggs, oil and flour.

2 When the dough begins to come together, start kneading it with both hands about 10 minutes, gradually pouring in 1 to 2 teaspoons water, until you form a malleable and firm dough that is not sticky. Wrap the dough in plastic wrap and leave to rest about 20 minutes.

3 Meanwhile, heat the sunflower oil in a heavy-bottomed saucepan over medium heat. Add the onion, cover and sweat 4 to 5 minutes until soft. Add the lamb, cinnamon, allspice, chili flakes and a little salt and cook 5 minutes longer until the meat browns. Set the pan aside.

4 Heat the oven to 400°F. Divide the dough in half. Working with one half at a time, flatten the dough on a lightly dusted countertop and roll it out to about ¹⁄₁₆ inch thick. Using a 4-inch round cookie cutter, stamp out 24 to 30 circles.

5 Place one circle in the palm of your hand, then place a generous teaspoonful of the meat mixture in the middle. Fold the dough over the filling and seal the edges to form a half-circle, then bring together the two edges of the half circle and seal tightly, leaving a hole in the middle. Place, sealed edges facing downward, on a lightly floured baking sheet. Repeat with the remaining circles and meat mixture. Bake in the oven 20 minutes or until lightly golden and crunchy.

6 Meanwhile, heat the yogurt in a heavy-bottomed saucepan over medium heat, then break in the remaining egg and mix well. Bring the mixture to a gentle boil, then reduce the heat to low and simmer 3 to 4 minutes, stirring continuously. The texture should be thick and creamy. If the mixture is too runny, dissolve the cornstarch in a little of the mixture, then stir it into the pan and mix until thicker.

7 Toast the pine nuts in a heavy-bottomed pan over medium heat for 1–2 minutes until golden and fragrant, shaking the pan often. Ladle the yogurt sauce into bowls, top with the tortellini and drizzle some Herb Butter over them. Sprinkle with the sumac and toasted pine nuts and serve with Vermicelli Rice, if you like.

Quinces Stuffed With Veal & Wheat Berries

SERVES 4
PREPARATION TIME: 25 minutes
COOKING TIME: 2 ¼ hours

juice and zest of 1 lemon, reserving the squeezed lemon shells

4 large quinces of similar size

2 cups wheat berries or rice

2 tablespoons vegetable oil, plus extra for greasing

1 onion, finely chopped

1 tablespoon peeled and very finely chopped gingerroot

3 garlic cloves, crushed

15 ounces ground veal

¼ teaspoon ground allspice

¼ teaspoon ground cinnamon

¼ teaspoon ground nutmeg

7 tablespoons verjuice, or lime juice to taste

7 tablespoons honey

1 teaspoon orange blossom water (optional)

7 tablespoons Greek yogurt

½ teaspoon Aleppo pepper flakes or crushed chili flakes

2 tablespoons almonds

chopped mint leaves, to sprinkle

sea salt and freshly ground black pepper

Undressed Herb Salad (see page 67), to serve

I have an infatuation with quince's hints of jasmine, guava and vanilla, which leave a lingering perfume on your fingers: aromas that intensify as the fruit cooks. You can use ground beef or lamb to make the stuffing if you prefer.

1 Pour plenty of water into a large mixing bowl and add the lemon juice and the squeezed lemon shells. Slice off and reserve the tops of the quinces, then scoop out and reserve the seeds and some pulp, leaving ½ inch of the peel. Add the hollowed-out quinces to the water.

2 Put the wheat berries in a heavy-bottomed saucepan over medium heat, cover with three times their volume in water and cook 1 hour, or until the berries are tender but still have a bite to them. Drain well.

3 Heat the oven to 350°F. Heat the oil in a heavy-bottomed pan over medium heat and sauté the onion 3 to 5 minutes until translucent. Add the ginger and 2 of the crushed garlic cloves and cook until aromatic. Add the reserved quince pulp and seeds, veal, allspice, cinnamon and nutmeg and cook 2 to 3 minutes longer. Pour in 3 tablespoons of the verjuice, add the cooked wheat berries and season to taste with salt and pepper, then mix thoroughly. Fill the cored quinces with the wheat berry mixture, replace the tops and place in a 6- to 8-inch lightly greased, round baking dish.

4 Put 1 cup plus 2 tablespoons water in a mixing bowl with the remaining verjuice and the lemon zest, honey and orange blossom water and season to taste with salt. Pour the mixture over the stuffed quinces, cover with foil and bake in the oven 1 hour, or until the quinces are soft, basting occasionally with the juices. Remove the quinces from the oven. If the juices are not thick like a pouring glaze, transfer them to a saucepan over medium heat and simmer to reduce farther.

5 Meanwhile, put the yogurt, Aleppo pepper, remaining garlic and salt in a blender and whiz the mixture about 1 minute until it's frothy.

6 Toast the almonds in a heavy-bottomed pan over medium heat 1 to 2 minutes until golden and fragrant, shaking the pan often.

7 Spoon 2 tablespoons of the yogurt into each of four shallow bowls, place a cooked quince on top, then drizzle a few spoonfuls of the thick juice over. Sprinkle with mint and the toasted almonds and serve with an Undressed Herb Salad.

eggplant, veal & yogurt crumble

SERVES 4
PREPARATION TIME: 25 minutes,
  plus making the bread
COOKING TIME: 50 minutes

4 teaspoons tahini

1 garlic bulb, cloves separated and
  finely chopped

3 tablespoons lemon juice

1¾ cups Greek yogurt at room
  temperature

3 tablespoons salted butter

2 onions, finely chopped

4 tablespoons pine nuts

14 ounces ground veal

2 teaspoons ground allspice

2 teaspoons Aleppo pepper flakes or
  crushed chili flakes

2 teaspoons dried mint

1 can (15-oz.) crushed tomatoes
  in juice

2 tablespoons pomegranate
  molasses

4 eggplants, about 2¼ pounds
  total weight

½ cup olive oil

2 small loaves stale Arabic Bread,
  roughly torn (see page 217)

chopped mint leaves, to sprinkle

pomegranate seeds (see page 216),
  to sprinkle

sea salt and freshly ground black
  pepper

This is a version of a dish known as fattet makdous. The word fatteh in Arabic means "tear or crumble" or "of crumbs," and traditionally stale bread is used as the base. If you prefer, you can use lamb or beef for this recipe.

1 Heat the oven to 400°F. Meanwhile, put the tahini, 1 teaspoon of the garlic, the lemon juice and 1 tablespoon water into a bowl and mix well. Add the yogurt and mix until the mixture forms a smooth, creamy texture. Season to taste with salt and pepper, then set aside at room temperature to let the flavors develop.

2 Melt the butter in a heavy-bottomed skillet over medium heat. Add the onions and cook about 4 minutes until soft and translucent. Add half the pine nuts and cook 1 to 2 minutes until lightly colored, then add the veal, allspice, Aleppo pepper flakes, dried mint and the remaining garlic and season to taste with salt and pepper. Mix well. Reduce the heat to low and cook until the meat is brown. Pour in the tomatoes and stir well to combine, then reduce the heat to low and cook 5 to 8 minutes. Remove the pan from the heat and pour in the pomegranate molasses, mixing well to incorporate. Cover and set aside.

3 Cut the eggplants in half lengthwise, keeping the stems intact, because they make moving the eggplants easier, as well as being more aesthetically pleasing. Transfer the eggplants to a baking sheet, skin-side down. Puncture the flesh of each eggplant a couple of times with a fork, taking care not to tear through the skin. Rub each eggplant half with 1 tablespoon of the oil and season to taste with salt and pepper. Bake in the oven about 20 minutes until the flesh is golden brown and soft.

4 Remove the eggplants from the oven (keep the oven on) and, using a fork, gently press down the flesh to mash. Transfer two eggplant halves to each of four plates. Put the Arabic bread on a cookie sheet and bake in the oven 2 to 3 minutes until golden, turning over halfway. Check the bread every minute to make sure it colors and crisps evenly.

5 Toast the remaining pine nuts in a heavy-bottomed pan over medium heat 1 to 2 minutes until golden and fragrant, shaking the pan often.

6 Assemble the eggplants by spooning 2 tablespoons of the meat and tomato mixture into each cavity and pouring 2 tablespoons of the yogurt dressing over. Crumble the toasted Arabic bread over, sprinkle with mint and pomegranate seeds and serve with the toasted pine nuts.

Veal Shoulder with butter beans

SERVES 4
PREPARATION TIME: 10 minutes,
  plus overnight soaking
COOKING TIME: 1 hour 40 minutes

1¾ cups dried butter beans, soaked
  overnight (see Cooking Chickpeas,
  page 215)

2 tablespoons sunflower oil

1 onion, finely chopped

10 ounces boneless veal or lamb
  shoulder, cut into 1½-inch cubes

1 garlic bulb, cloves separated and
  crushed with the blade of a knife

2 or 3 marrow bones (optional)

1 teaspoon ground cinnamon

1 teaspoon ground allspice

⅔ cup tomato paste

sea salt and freshly ground black
  pepper

Vermicelli Rice (see page 215),
  to serve

warm Arabic Bread (see page 217),
  to serve

This stew conjures up memories of my grandmother, after-school dinners on a dark, winter's evening and fighting over the last bone, then pounding it heavily on the cutting board, being careful not to let a single drop of marrow escape. I have listed the bones as optional, but for me, the highlight of this dish has always been "inhaling" the rich marrow, so pleasing in its texture and gentle nutty sweetness. If you do want to cook the meat on the bone, ask your butcher to chop the bones into smaller pieces, and then add them with the butter beans. When the dish is served, use a marrow spoon to extract the marrow.

1 Drain the soaked butter beans, rinse well and set aside.

2 Heat the oil in a saucepan and add the onion. Cover, then sweat over medium heat 4 to 5 minutes, stirring often until the onions are soft and translucent. Add the veal and sear 3 to 5 minutes until brown on all sides.

3 Add the garlic, butter beans, marrow bones, if using, cinnamon and allspice and cover with 5 cups water. Increase the heat to high and bring to a boil, then reduce the heat to medium-low, cover with a lid and leave to simmer about 1 hour.

4 Add the tomato paste and season to taste with salt and pepper. (Don't add salt before this stage, because it can extend the cooking time of the beans.) Cover and cook 30 minutes longer, or until the butter beans are soft, the meat is tender and the sauce reduces and thickens. Serve with Vermicelli Rice and warm Arabic Bread.

Oxtail with Oozing Okra

SERVES 4 to 6
PREPARATION TIME: 35 minutes,
  plus making the harissa and stock
  (optional)
COOKING TIME: 1 hour

1¾ pounds tomatoes

12 ounces oxtail

1 teaspoon paprika

½ teaspoon ground cinnamon

5 tablespoons sunflower oil

1 large onion, thinly sliced

3 garlic cloves, finely chopped

2-inch piece gingerroot, peeled and
  grated

1 cardamom pod, crushed

2 cups small potatoes cut in half

¼ teaspoon Harissa (see page 210)

4 ready-to-eat dried apricots,
  halved

3 cups Vegetable Stock (optional,
  see page 211)

12 ounces baby okra

1 handful cilantro leaves, finely
  chopped

sea salt

Couscous (see page 216), to serve

There are variations of this dish across North Africa and the Middle East, as well as a multitude of other cuisines, and its health benefits are many. You can reduce the sliminess of okra by soaking it in a vinegar solution, or by frying it. When you wash okra, dry it and any surface it will touch, including the knife, and always trim it without puncturing. Try to use very small okra if you can find them. If you prefer to bake the dish, toss the okra in 2 tablespoons olive oil first and bake at 350°F about 10 minutes.

1 With a sharp knife, cut a cross in the skin of each tomato, then put them in a heatproof bowl and cover with boiling water. Leave to stand 2 to 3 minutes or until the skin peels, then drain. Plunge into cold water to stop the cooking, then peel off the skins and discard. Slice each tomato in half and scoop out the seeds, then finely chop the flesh.

2 Rub the oxtail with salt, paprika and cinnamon. Heat 2 tablespoons of the oil in a heavy-bottomed saucepan over medium heat, then add the oxtail and fry until brown, then remove, cover and set aside.

3 Add the onion to the pan, cover and sweat 2 to 3 minutes until soft and translucent. Add the garlic, ginger and cardamom and cook 1 minute longer, or until aromatic. Add the potatoes, toss to cover and cook 1 minute, then return the meat to the pan, add the prepared tomatoes, harissa and apricots and cover with vegetable stock or water. Bring to a boil over high heat, then lower the heat and simmer 45 minutes, or until the meat is tender and the potatoes are cooked. Alternatively, remove the meat from the pan, slice around the bone, chop the meat into rough cubes and return to the pan with the bones.

4 Meanwhile, wash the okra under running water to remove any grit and pat completely dry with paper towels. Prepare the okra using a paring knife to shave off the crown, diagonally, into a fine point, being sure not to break the okra open at any point, or you will have more of the mucilaginous substance released. Heat the remaining oil in a skillet over medium heat, then, once the oil is hot, add the prepared okra and cilantro and fry 8 to 10 minutes until bright green and cooked, being sure not to brown them. Transfer to the stew and cook 5 minutes longer. Serve with Couscous.

seafood

almond-crusted scallops

SERVES 4
PREPARATION TIME: 10 minutes,
  plus making the preserved lemon
COOKING TIME: 10 minutes

1 cup very finely ground blanched
  almonds

1 teaspoon ground mahlab (optional)

2 eggs

16 scallops, about 1 pound 2 ounces
  total weight

4 tablespoons sunflower oil

½ cup verjuice, or lime juice to taste

7 tablespoons cold salted butter,
  diced

2 wedges Preserved Lemon (see
  page 212), peels rinsed and finely
  chopped

⅓ cup dates, pitted and roughly
  chopped

sea salt

Couscous (see page 216), to serve

Fattoush Salad (see page 61),
  Undressed Herb Salad (see page
  67) or Shaved Beet, Radish
  & Grapefruit Salad (see page 62),
  to serve

*These plump scallops are inspired by North African flavors,
and their gentle sweetness is highlighted by the dates, nutty
almonds and subtle fragrance of mahlab. The sharpness of the
preserved lemons and verjuice works well to balance it out,
and the buttery goodness is always welcome.*

1 Put the ground almonds and mahlab, if using, in a large mixing bowl,
mix well and season to taste with salt.

2 Break the eggs into another bowl and whisk well. Toss the scallops
in the whisked egg to coat. Remove them from the egg, shaking them to
remove any excess egg, then add them to the ground almond mixture.
Toss again to coat.

3 Heat the oil in a skillet over medium heat (the oil should not be so hot
that it's smoking) and sear the scallops about 2 minutes on each side
until golden brown and just cooked through. The flesh will be bouncy
when pushed, and if you slice one open, it will be a soft pinky-white.
A good scallop should be tender and juicy so it's important not
to overcook them.

4 Remove the scallops from the pan, transfer them to a warm plate
and cover. Add the verjuice to the pan, scraping up the brown bits and
simmering the mixture 2 to 3 minutes to reduce it.

5 Reduce the heat to medium-low and add the butter, one piece
at a time, whisking to create a creamy consistency. Increase the heat
to medium-high and let the butter foam as you continue to whisk. Once
it starts to turn brown, quickly remove the pan from the heat before the
butter begins to burn. Add the scallops, preserved lemon and dates and
toss well to coat. Serve with Couscous and one or more of the salads.

mussels in arak

4½ pounds fresh mussels

3 tablespoons salted butter

2 shallots, very finely chopped

1 cup Arak or Pernod

1 cup dry white wine

2 tomatoes, very finely chopped

4 garlic cloves, finely chopped

1 bay leaf

juice of 1½ lemons

3 tablespoons tarragon leaves, finely chopped, plus extra for sprinkling

sea salt and freshly ground black pepper

warm Arabic Bread (see page 217) or Potato Matchsticks (see page 218), to serve

Arak, very much the national drink in Lebanon, is nicknamed the "milk of lions," most probably because when mixed with water to serve, it turns a milky white, but also because it was drunk by men, sometimes in the mornings, to show off their strength and masculinity. Arak is not traditionally used for cooking, but it works wonderfully in this dish, which has a double hit of anise from the Arak (use Pernod, if you prefer) and tarragon. The flavor mellows nicely, leaving behind only the slightest hint of anise.

1 Wash the mussels under cold running water, pulling off any beards from the shells (this should be done with a gentle pull in the direction of the "hinge"). Only do this just before cooking, because this process can injure or kill the mussel, which is why some might not open after cooking. Scrape off any barnacles using the back of a sharp knife and discard any open mussels that don't close when given a sharp tap on the countertop.

2 Melt the butter in a large, deep, heavy-bottomed saucepan over medium-low heat. Add the shallots, cover and sweat 3 to 4 minutes until soft and translucent. Pour in the Arak and wine and add the tomatoes, garlic, bay leaf, lemon juice, tarragon and salt and pepper to taste, then stir and simmer about 2 minutes until the liquid reduces by half. Taste and adjust the seasoning, if needed.

3 Add ½ cup water if you find the broth too reduced, then add the mussels. Cover and cook 3 to 4 minutes, shaking the pan gently, until all the mussels open. Don't overcook mussels, because they turn dry and tough. Discard any mussels that are not open. Sprinkle with extra tarragon and serve with warm Arabic Bread or Potato Matchsticks.

slow-braised spiced squid

SERVES 4
PREPARATION TIME: 30 minutes,
  plus making the spice mixture
COOKING TIME: 2 hours

4 tablespoons salted butter

1 onion, finely chopped

4 cleaned squid, about 2 pounds
  4 ounces total weight, tentacles
  reserved

2 ¼ pounds tomatoes

14 ounces fennel bulbs

8 garlic cloves, finely chopped

1 small hot red chili, seeded and
  finely chopped

½ cup coarse bulgur wheat
  (grade 3 or 4), rinsed

3 tablespoons finely chopped dill
  leaves, plus extra for sprinkling

⅔ cup Arak, ouzo or Pernod

¼ teaspoon Lebanese Seven Spices
  (see page 211)

2 cups plus 2 tablespoons fish stock

juice of 1 lemon (optional)

2 tablespoons olive oil

sumac, for dusting

sea salt and freshly ground black
  pepper

lemon wedges, to serve

Standing apart from much of the Levant and the rest of Palestine, the people of Gaza have an affection for heat, with chili and dill forming one of the cuisine's sacred combinations. This squid recipe is another example of the Levant's flair for stuffing, and while the recipe calls for bulgur, rice can also be used. Although not traditional, I have added fennel and a generous drizzle of Arak.

1 To make the stuffing, melt half the butter in a wide, heavy-based saucepan over high heat. Add the onion, reduce the heat to medium-low and cook about 5 minutes until the onion is soft and translucent.

2 Chop the tentacles into ¾-inch pieces. Chop one-quarter of the tomatoes and one of the fennel bulbs.

3 Add the tentacles, garlic, chili and chopped fennel to the pan and cook 1 minute, or until fragrant, stirring once. Mix in the chopped tomatoes, bulgur wheat, 4 tablespoons water, 2 tablespoons of the dill, 3 tablespoons of the Arak and the spice mixture and heat through, stirring. Season to taste with salt and pepper. Set aside until the mixture is cool enough to handle.

4 Meanwhile, cut the remaining tomatoes and fennel bulbs into quarters.

5 Stuff each squid cavity two-thirds full with one-quarter of the squid and tomato stuffing, then secure with wooden toothpicks.

6 Heat the oven to 250°F. Put the remaining butter in a 12-inch ovenproof pan deep enough to hold the stock over high heat. When the butter melts, add the stuffed squid and sear on each side 1 to 2 minutes. Pour in ½ cup of the Arak and let the mixture simmer over low heat 5 minutes, or until it reduces by half. Add the quartered tomatoes and fennel, pour in the fish stock and sprinkle in the remaining dill and any remaining stuffing. Cover with foil and cook in the oven 1½ hours. Remove the foil for the last 30 minutes of cooking to reduce the liquid slightly. During the last 10 minutes of cooking, change the oven setting to broil (or heat a separate broiler and move the pan into it). Put the pan under the broiler 10 minutes until the squid is soft and tender.

7 Add the remaining Arak, lemon juice, if using, and oil to the pan, season to taste with salt and pepper, then sprinkle with dill. Transfer the stuffed squid to plates, spoon the Arak sauce over and dust with sumac. Serve with lemon wedges for squeezing over.

Shrimp, spinach & bread crumble

SERVES 4
PREPARATION TIME: 25 minutes,
  plus making the bread
COOKING TIME: 25 minutes

2 loaves stale Arabic Bread
  (see page 217), roughly crumbled

2 tablespoons sumac

2 tablespoons olive oil

7 tablespoons salted butter

1 large onion, finely chopped

1 garlic bulb, cloves separated and
  finely chopped or crushed

1 small hot red chili, finely chopped
  (optional)

2 pounds large raw shrimp, shelled
  and deveined

1 cup Arak or Pernod

6 tomatoes, finely chopped

2 handfuls cilantro leaves,
  finely chopped

3 handfuls spinach leaves,
  finely chopped

juice of 1 lemon

sea salt and freshly ground black
  pepper

This dish resembles a Greek shrimp saganaki or a shrimp vindaloo, but it's really my take on a similar dish my father prepares. I've turned it into another crumble (like the Eggplant, Veal & Yogurt Crumble on page 119), by tossing in crisp Arabic bread crumbs to soak up the all-important juices. I've also added a lacing of Arak to give it a more intoxicating flavor.

1 Heat the oven to 350°F. Put the bread pieces on a baking sheet. Sprinkle with sumac, drizzle the oil over and toss to combine. Bake in the oven 10 minutes, shaking the sheet a couple of times, until the bread pieces are crisp and golden.

2 Meanwhile, melt 4 tablespoons of the butter in a heavy-bottomed saucepan over medium heat. Add the onion, cover and sweat 5 minutes, or until soft and translucent. Add the garlic, chili, if using, and shrimp and toss to coat, then sear the shrimp about 2 minutes on each side until they are light pink. Remove the shrimp, cover and set aside.

3 Add the Arak to the pan and leave to bubble and reduce 2 to 3 minutes to reduce. Add the tomatoes and cilantro and cook 4 to 5 minutes until the tomatoes are soft. Add the spinach leaves, the shrimp and the remaining butter, season to taste with salt and pepper and toss to combine, cooking 3 to 4 minutes until the spinach wilts and the shrimp are just cooked through. Squeeze the lemon juice over. Remove the pan from the heat and transfer the shrimp and other ingredients to bowls. Sprinkle the crisp bread crumbs over and serve.

Spiced Shrimp & Coconut Rice

SERVES 4
PREPARATION TIME: 45 minutes,
  plus making the rice
COOKING TIME: 45 minutes

2 tablespoons unsalted butter

1 onion, finely chopped

1 small hot red chili, seeded and
finely chopped

½ teaspoon ground cinnamon

1 ¼-inch piece gingerroot, peeled
and finely chopped

2 teaspoons tomato paste

1 teaspoon ground turmeric
(optional)

1 teaspoon ground fenugreek
(optional)

1 pound 2 ounces large raw shrimp,
shelled and deveined

5 garlic cloves, crushed

2 small handfuls cilantro leaves,
finely chopped, plus extra for
sprinkling

1 cup plus 2 tablespoons coconut
cream

zest and juice of 1 lime,
  or 2 teaspoons dried lime powder

6 tablespoons sunflower oil

1 recipe quantity Parboiled Rice (see
page 214)

sea salt and freshly ground black
pepper

lime wedges, to serve

*This rice dish packs a little more heat than one would expect
from Persian cuisine. Hailing from southern Iran, it's a great
example of the Indian influences on the Persian Gulf, following
a rich history of trade. This recipe strays from tradition with
the addition of coconut cream.*

1 Melt the butter in a skillet over medium heat. Add the onion and
fry 3 to 5 minutes until soft and translucent. Add the chili, cinnamon,
ginger and tomato paste, plus the turmeric and fenugreek, if using,
and cook, stirring, 2 to 3 minutes longer.

2 Add the shrimp, garlic and cilantro, stirring briefly so they are
covered in the spice-and-herb mixture, then cook 2 minutes. Remove
the pan from the heat. Mix in the coconut cream and lime zest and
juice. Season to taste with salt and pepper.

3 Heat the oil in a heavy-bottomed saucepan over medium heat until
it's sizzling. Using a spoon, sprinkle 4 or 5 tablespoons of the rice across
the bottom of the pan to cover. Add 2 or 3 tablespoons of the shrimp
and coconut mixture and continue creating alternate layers of shrimp
mixture and rice, building the mixture up into a dome shape. Finish
with a layer of rice. (Tipping all the rice in at once will squash and
compress it, and the end result will not be as light and fluffy.)

4 Using the handle of a wooden spoon, make three holes in the rice
all the way to the bottom of the pan.

5 Wrap the saucepan lid in a clean dish towel and tie it into a tight
knot at the handle, then use it to cover the pan as tightly as you can
so steam does not escape. (The dish towel prevents the moisture from
dripping into the rice, making it soggy.) Cook the rice over medium
heat 2 to 3 minutes until the rice is steaming (you will see puffs of steam
escaping at the edge of the lid), then reduce the heat to low and cook
20 to 25 minutes, with the lid on all the time.

6 Serve the rice and tahdeeg (crisp bottom) following the directions in
steps 5–7 of Steamed Rice on page 214. Sprinkle with extra cilantro and
serve with lime wedges.

sea bass with spiced caramelized onion rice

SERVES 4
PREPARATION TIME: 20 minutes
COOKING TIME: 50 minutes

whole sea bass, about 1 pound
  2 ounces, dressed and scaled with
  the head left on

½ cup sunflower oil

4 onions, thinly sliced

2 tablespoons ground cumin

1 teaspoon ground cinnamon

1 teaspoon ground allspice

1 cup medium-grain rice

2 tablespoons pine nuts

2 tablespoons olive oil

3 tablespoons finely chopped
  parsley leaves (optional)

sea salt and freshly ground black
  pepper

lemon wedges, to serve

Tarator (see page 220), to serve

This fragrant dish called seeyadeeyeh is a family favorite. It was handed down to my Aunt Amale via my grandmother, finally making its way into my repertoire. My grandmother grew up along the coast of Batroun, where her family's picturesque restaurant, Jammal, still stands overlooking the water grottos where she once swam. This recipe is a homage to her sea-loving soul.

1 Cut off the fish head and season it with salt. Set aside the remaining fish. Heat the sunflower oil in a heavy-bottomed skillet over medium heat. When the oil begins to sizzle, add the fish head and fry about 5 minutes on each side. Remove the fish head and set aside.

2 Add the onions to the pan and fry about 5 minutes until golden, stirring occasionally. Remove the pan from the heat and transfer the onions to a plate lined with paper towels. Spread three-quarters of the drained onions evenly across the bottom of a heavy-bottomed saucepan. Place the pan over low heat, add the fish head and cover with 2 ¼ cups water. Add the cumin, cinnamon and allspice, then season to taste with salt. Cover, increase the heat to medium-high and bring to a boil, then remove the fish head and reserve.

3 Add the rice to the pan, reduce the heat to low and cook, covered, about 30 minutes until the rice is tender and the water has been absorbed.

4 Heat the oven to 400°F. Meanwhile, toast the pine nuts in a heavy-bottomed pan over medium heat 1 to 2 minutes until golden and fragrant, shaking the pan often.

5 Put the uncooked fish in a baking dish, season to taste with salt and pepper and drizzle with the olive oil. Bake 20 minutes, or until the fish flakes easily when pushed with a fork. Divide the fish into four equal portions.

6 Transfer the cooked rice to a dish, stand the fish head in the middle, if you like, and arrange the fish portions on top of the rice. Add the remaining caramelized onions and the toasted pine nuts to the dish. Sprinkle the parsley over, if using, and serve the dish with lemon wedges and Tarator.

Veiled sea bass with a spicy surprise

SERVES 4
PREPARATION TIME: 20 minutes,
  plus making the preserved lemon
COOKING TIME: 25 minutes

1 handful parsley leaves

1 handful cilantro leaves

2 tablespoons finely chopped
  dill leaves

1 tablespoon peeled and roughly
  chopped gingerroot

1 mild red chili, seeded and roughly
  chopped

1 wedge Preserved Lemon (see
  page 212), peel rinsed and roughly
  chopped

8 garlic cloves, crushed with the
  blade of a knife

¼ teaspoon ground cumin

6 tablespoons olive oil, plus extra
  for greasing

4 sea bass, about 3 pounds in total,
  scaled and dressed with the heads
  intact

12 large bottled grape leaves, rinsed

sea salt and freshly ground black
  pepper

Couscous (see page 216), to serve

lemon wedges, to serve

The inspiration for "veiling" these sea bass came from chef Greg Malouf, who "veils" quails with grape leaves. As I had an excess of bottled grape leaves, and a few sea bass thawing, it seemed appropriate to marry them. The grape leaves lock the moisture in as the fish is steamed and they also lend a very subtle sweetness. If using fresh grape leaves, blanch them in boiling water for a minute, or until pliable.

1 Heat the oven to 375°F and lightly grease a baking sheet with oil. Put the parsley, cilantro, dill, ginger, chili, preserved lemon, garlic and cumin in a blender and pulse several times until you've made a rough paste, stopping to scrape the side down as needed. Pour in 4 tablespoons of the oil and pulse once more to combine. Spoon the mixture into the fish cavities.

2 Season the sea bass with salt and pepper and rub with the remaining oil. Wrap each sea bass with 3 grape leaves, starting at the head and working all the way down, but leaving the tail exposed. Put the fish, seam-side down, on the baking sheet and roast 20 to 25 minutes, depending on the size of the fish (the general rule is 7 minutes cooking time per 1 inch measured at the thickest part of the fish), until the fish is tender and cooked through. Serve with Couscous and lemon wedges.

Salmon with herby butter and barberries

SERVES 4
PREPARATION TIME: 30 minutes,
  plus making the saffron liquid
COOKING TIME: 30 minutes

4 tablespoons salted butter, soft,
  plus extra for greasing

½ cup dried barberries or
  cranberries

3 handfuls parsley leaves,
  finely chopped

3 handfuls cilantro leaves,
  finely chopped

2 handfuls tarragon leaves,
  finely chopped

2 handfuls dill leaves, finely chopped

6 garlic cloves, very finely chopped

⅓ cup walnut pieces, coarsely
  chopped

2 tablespoons Saffron Liquid (see
  page 212)

2 tablespoons pomegranate
  molasses

1 salmon, about 3 pounds 5 ounces,
  scaled, butterflied and skin scored
  with the head intact

sea salt and freshly ground black
  pepper

Chelow Rice (see page 214), to serve

lemon or lime wedges, to serve

This is an ideal dish for a lavish dinner party, exuding buttery goodness with a balance of herbs, sweet and tangy barberries and a pleasant hint of nuttiness from the walnuts, all coming together to create a parade of flavors. You can also use haddock, cod or sea bass.

1 Heat the oven to 350°F and grease a baking sheet with butter.

2 Put the barberries in a bowl and cover with water, then leave to soak 5 minutes. Drain well and pat dry with a dish towel.

3 In a bowl, mix the herbs, garlic, drained barberries, walnuts, saffron liquid, 3 tablespoons of the butter and the pomegranate molasses to create a paste. Season with salt and pepper to taste.

4 Rub the interior and exterior of the fish with some salt and stuff the fish with the butter-and-herb paste. Sew up the fish cavity using a needle and thread or secure with 3 or 4 wooden toothpicks.

5 Melt the remaining butter in a small saucepan. Baste the fish with the butter and season with pepper.

6 Bake, uncovered, 25 to 30 minutes, depending on the size of the fish (the general rule is 7 minutes cooking time per 1 inch measured at the thickest part of the fish), until the fish is tender, cooked through and the flesh flakes easily. Remove the fish from the oven and transfer it to a platter. Drizzle with the cooking juices and serve with Chelow Rice and lemon wedges.

tamarind & herb mackerel stew

SERVES 4
PREPARATION TIME: 30 minutes,
  plus soaking
COOKING TIME: 1 hour

9 ounces tamarind pulp, from
  a block

4 tablespoons sunflower oil

1 large onion, finely chopped

1 teaspoon ground turmeric

1 small hot red chili, seeded and
  finely chopped

1 tablespoon dried fenugreek

4 handfuls cilantro leaves, finely
  chopped

1 handful parsley leaves, finely
  chopped

1 garlic bulb, cloves separated and
  finely chopped or crushed

2¼ pounds mackerel fillets, cut into
  1-inch-thick steaks

sea salt and freshly ground black
  pepper

Chelow Rice (see page 214), to serve

I find tamarind to be quite underrated. It's a souring agent that lends a very distinctive flavor to curries and stews, such as this wonderfully rich and pungent dish from the Persian Gulf region of Iran. Tamarind is sold in several forms and can be found in major supermarkets, as well as in Asian, Spanish and Middle Eastern grocery stores. I prefer to use it in block form, rather than concentrate, since it's nearly identical to fresh pods, but easier to use, because you don't have to break it out of its shell. It's also more tart and flavorful. If you prefer, you can use cod, haddock or tuna in this recipe.

1 Put the tamarind pulp in a large heatproof bowl, pour 2¼ cups boiling water over and leave to soak about 10 minutes. With a fork or your hands, mash the tamarind until it "dissolves" and you are left with a light brown, thick, saucelike paste. Strain through a fine strainer, discarding the seeds and tough fibers. (Tamarind can be prepared as described here and stored in an airtight container in the refrigerator up to 2 weeks.)

2 Heat half the oil in a large, heavy-bottomed saucepan over medium-low heat. Add the onion and fry 3 minutes, or until translucent and light brown. Add the turmeric, chili and fenugreek and cook 3 to 4 minutes longer until aromatic. Add the cilantro, parsley and garlic and cook 2 to 3 minutes until the herbs wilt and darken in color, stirring often. Add the tamarind paste and simmer, partially covered, 30 minutes.

3 Meanwhile, season the mackerel with salt and pepper. Heat a heavy-bottomed skillet over medium-low heat. Add the remaining oil and fry the fish 4 to 5 minutes on each side until golden brown. As each fillet is fried, transfer it to a plate lined with paper towels to drain.

4 Add the fish to the herb-and-tamarind mixture in the saucepan and simmer, uncovered, over low heat about 20 minutes until the liquid reduces and thickens. The fish should flake easily when pushed with a fork. Season to taste with salt and pepper and serve with Chelow Rice.

spicy snapper in the tripoli manner

SERVES 4
PREPARATION TIME: 20 minutes,
  plus making the tarator
COOKING TIME: 40 minutes

1 whole red snapper, 4½ pounds,
  dressed

2 tablespoons olive oil

1 onion, quartered

3 mild red chilies, tops sliced off

8 garlic cloves, crushed with the
  blade of a knife

1 teaspoon ground allspice

1 teaspoon ground cinnamon

1 teaspoon sea salt, plus extra
  for seasoning

3 handfuls cilantro leaves, plus extra
  to serve

½ cup chopped walnuts

3 tomatoes, finely chopped

⅓ cup pine nuts

1 recipe quantity Tarator (see
  page 220)

freshly ground black pepper

Vermicelli Rice (see page 215),
  to serve

lemon wedges, to serve

Known as samkeh harra, this is a speciality of the port city of Tripoli in the north of Lebanon, where you'll even find the mixture turned into a paste and wrapped in Arabic bread as a sandwich. The color contrast of the red snapper against the creamy tahini with flecks of herbs makes for a visually appealing dish.

1 Heat the oven to 400°F. Put the fish on a baking sheet, season with salt and pepper to taste and drizzle with the oil. Cover with foil and roast 30 to 40 minutes, depending on the size of the fish (the general rule is 7 minutes cooking time per 1 inch measured at the thickest part of the fish), until the fish is golden and tender.

2 Meanwhile, put the onion, chilies, garlic, allspice, cinnamon and salt in a food processor and pulse 1 minute. Add the cilantro and pulse again 1 to 2 minutes longer until a thick, cohesive paste develops. Transfer the paste to a heavy-bottomed skillet over medium heat. Add the walnuts and tomatoes, stir well and cook about 5 minutes until the mixture is fragrant.

3 While the garlic and cilantro paste is cooking, toast the pine nuts in a heavy-bottomed pan over medium heat 1 to 2 minutes until golden and fragrant, shaking the pan often. Set aside.

4 Pour the tarator over the garlic and cilantro paste, mix well to combine and cook 1 to 2 minutes until warm.

5 Transfer the fish to a large serving dish, being careful to keep it in one piece, then pour about half the dressing over the cooked fish, reserving the rest for serving on the side. Sprinkle the fish with the toasted pine nuts and extra cilantro leaves and serve with the Vermicelli Rice and lemon wedges.

blackened sea bream

SERVES 4
PREPARATION TIME: 10 minutes,
  plus marinating
COOKING TIME: 45 minutes

4 whole sea bream, pollock
  or haddock, about 2¾ pounds
  total weight, dressed and
  butterflied with head and tail
  intact

2 tablespoons smoked sea salt
  flakes

1 tablespoon tamarind paste
  or lemon juice

3 tablespoons olive oil

1 tablespoon ground dried lime
  (optional)

chopped cilantro leaves, to sprinkle

sea salt and freshly ground black
  pepper

Chelow Rice (see page 214)
  or Vermicelli Rice (see page 215),
  to serve

Burned Tomato & Chili Jam
  (optional, see page 219), to serve

FOR THE GREEN MANGO
  CHUTNEY
2 green mangoes, sliced into
  ½-inch cubes

1¼-inch piece gingerroot, peeled
  and finely chopped or grated

½ garlic clove, finely chopped
  or crushed

½ teaspoon turmeric

¼ teaspoon ground fenugreek

a small pinch dried chili flakes

4 tablespoons apple cider vinegar

2 tablespoons honey

a small pinch sea salt

The infamous masqouf, as Iraq's national dish is known, is a much-revered dish for Iraqis, reserved for special occasions. Considered to be food for the mind as well as the body, this Baghdad specialty sprang up along the banks of the Tigris, where the day's catch would be served to Arak-sozzled patrons in the cafés. It's traditionally prepared with freshwater fish, similar to carp, butterflied and hung on skewers over brushwood fires. Mango chutney was introduced via Indian traders, and Iraqis made it their own with the inclusion of spices such as fenugreek. You may need 2 large grilling baskets.

1 Put all the fish in a grill pan and season the interiors and exteriors generously with the smoked salt.

2 Put the tamarind paste in a mixing bowl, add 3 tablespoons water and mix well. Add the oil and dried lime, if using, and whisk well. Season to taste with black pepper. Baste each of the fish liberally all over with the tamarind marinade. Cover and set aside 30 minutes.

3 Meanwhile, prepare the mango chutney. Put the mangoes, ginger, garlic, turmeric, fenugreek, chili flakes, vinegar, honey, salt and 1½ cups water in a heavy-bottomed saucepan over medium heat. Cover and bring to a boil, then reduce the heat to low and simmer 20 to 25 minutes until the mango is soft and most of the liquid evaporates. The chutney should be slightly runny.

4 Depending on your choice, heat a broiler to high, heat a charcoal barbecue until the charcoal is burning white or turn on a gas barbecue. Secure the fish by flattening them between the wire racks of large fish-grilling baskets, 2 fish per basket, then cook 7 minutes on each side, or until charred, crisp and flaky. Alternatively, heat the oven to 350°F and bake the fish on wire racks placed above baking sheets 10 to 15 minutes, depending on the size of the fish (the general rule is 7 minutes cooking time per 1 inch measured at the thickest part of the fish).

5 If using fillets, then heat a shallow, nonstick skillet over medium heat and sear the fish 5 minutes on each side, carefully turning them.

6 Sprinkle cilantro over the fish and serve with Chelow Rice, along with the mango chutney and Burned Tomato and Chili Jam, if you like.

monkfish tagine with chermoula

SERVES 4
PREPARATION TIME: 15 minutes,
 plus marinating and making the
 chermoula, saffron and preserved
 lemon
COOKING TIME: 1 ¼ hours

4 monkfish fillets, about 1 pound
 2 ounces total weight

1 recipe quantity Chermoula
 (see page 210)

2 to 3 tablespoons olive oil

1 onion, thinly sliced

1 ½ cups sliced tomatoes, sliced

2 cups thinly sliced large potatoes

½ cup thinly sliced pitted prunes

a pinch ground saffron (see page
 212)

2 wedges Preserved Lemon, peel
 rinsed (see page 212)

1 bay leaf

Couscous (see page 216), to serve

This is very loosely based on a recipe by Claudia Roden. Use any kind of meaty fish that can withstand the lengthy cooking time, which renders the fish soft and moist. I use a tagine pot to cook this, but if you don't have one, use a heavy-bottomed baking dish.

1 Put the monkfish in a bowl and spread half the chermoula over the top. Cover and leave to marinate in the refrigerator 2 hours.

2 When you are ready to cook, heat the oven to 300°F. If you are using a tagine dish, season it first by rubbing 1 tablespoon of the oil over the inside.

3 Lay half the onion, tomato, potato and prune slices over the bottom, then lay the marinated monkfish fillets on top. Season with the saffron, add the preserved lemon wedges and the bay leaf, then repeat the layer of sliced vegetables and prunes. Cover with 1 cup plus 2 tablespoons water, put the lid on and cook 1 hour.

4 Remove the dish from the oven. Put the remaining oil and one-third of the remaining chermoula in a bowl and mix well. Drizzle this mixture over the tagine. Return the dish to the oven to cook, uncovered, 15 minutes longer. Serve the tagine hot, with the remaining chermoula either drizzled over it or served on the side, accompanied by Couscous.

vegetarian

pan-fried squares

SERVES 4
PREPARATION TIME: 40 minutes
  plus resting
COOKING TIME: 35 minutes

¾ cup all-purpose flour, sifted

¾ cup fine semolina

½ teaspoon sugar

½ teaspoon sea salt, plus extra
  for seasoning

¼ teaspoon active dry yeast

6 tablespoons olive oil, plus extra
  for greasing

1 red onion, thinly sliced

1 yellow bell pepper, seeded and
  thinly sliced

1 apple

juice of ½ lemon

6 sundried tomatoes in oil, drained
  and thinly sliced

4 ounces soft goat cheese

2 tablespoons salted butter

freshly ground black pepper

Pomegranate & Cucumber Salad
  (see page 64), to serve

Undressed Herb Salad (optional, see
  page 67), to serve

These crepelike semolina packages are prepared using dough patiently stretched to paper-thin thickness, stuffed and then folded into squares. The apple lends moisture and gentle sweetness. The cheese quantity can be increased to taste.

1 Put the flour, semolina, sugar and salt in a mixing bowl and combine with a fork. Put ½ cup warm water in a small bowl, sprinkle the yeast over and mix well, then gradually pour the liquid over the flour mixture as you mix it into a dough.

2 Knead the dough 15 minutes, or until you achieve a very smooth, elastic and malleable dough that is soft, but not sticky. Shape the dough into a ball, drizzle 1 tablespoon of the oil over your hands and then grease the dough ball. Return the dough to the bowl, cover with a damp dish towel and leave to rest about 10 minutes.

3 Meanwhile, prepare the filling. Heat 2 tablespoons of the oil in a skillet over medium heat. Add the onion and cook 5 minutes until light golden. Add the pepper and cook 3 to 4 minutes until soft, but with a slight bite to it. Core and slice the apple into thin wedges, then sprinkle it with the lemon juice to stop it discoloring. Add the apple to the pan with the sundried tomatoes. Toss everything together and cook 1 minute longer. Remove the pan from the heat and leave to cool, then crumble the goat cheese over and season to taste with salt and pepper.

4 Lightly grease a cookie sheet with more of the oil and divide the dough into four equal portions, each about the size of a golf ball. Using your fingers, begin to spread one of the dough balls outward into a very thin, almost transparent circle, 10 to 12 inches in diameter, using a little bit of the remaining oil as required, and then dot with one-quarter of the butter.

5 Divide the filling into four equal portions. Spoon one-quarter of the prepared filling into the middle of the dough circle. Fold one-third of the circle into the middle and repeat the same with the opposing side. Now fold each open end into the middle to achieve a square with the filling secure between the layers. Transfer the prepared dough square to the cookie sheet. Repeat steps 4 and 5 with the remaining dough and filling.

6 Put a heavy-bottomed, nonstick skillet over medium heat. Add the squares one at a time, flattening each one with the palm of your hand, and cook 4 to 5 minutes on each side until crisp and golden. Serve with the salads, if you like.

falafel & tarator wraps

SERVES 4
PREPARATION TIME: 30 minutes,
  plus soaking and draining the
  chickpeas, and making the bread
  and tarator
COOKING TIME: 10 minutes

1 ¼ cups dried chickpeas, soaked
  overnight (see page 215)

1 onion, quartered

2 garlic cloves, crushed with the
  blade of a knife

½ green bell pepper, seeded

1 handful mint leaves

1 handful parsley leaves

1 handful cilantro leaves

1 teaspoon sea salt, plus extra
  for seasoning

1 teaspoon ground allspice

½ teaspoon ground cumin

½ teaspoon baking soda

1 tablespoon all-purpose flour,
  if needed

sunflower oil, for deep-frying

4–6 small loaves Arabic Bread (see
  page 217)

shredded lettuce

Tarator (see page 220)

1 onion, thinly sliced (optional)

1 tomato, thinly sliced (optional)

pickles, banana peppers, turnips
  and beets, thinly sliced (optional)

1 handful parsley leaves,
  finely chopped

freshly ground black pepper

*It's commonly believed that falafel originated millennia ago
in Egypt, where they were prepared using a mixture of broad
beans and chickpeas. I prefer to stick with chickpeas, but don't
be tempted to use canned chickpeas, as they will fall apart.*

1 Drain the chickpeas well and leave in a colander 2 hours to remove
as much moisture as possible, shaking the colander every once in a
while. Alternatively, a faster approach is to use a salad spinner, if you
have one: add the chickpeas, close and spin 2 or 3 times to remove the
excess moisture. Set the chickpeas aside.

2 Put the onion, garlic, pepper, herbs, salt and spices into a food
processor and whiz 1 to 2 minutes until blended into a rough paste
(it should not be too smooth or the batter will fall apart during cooking).
Squeeze out any excess water and discard it. Return the paste to the
food processor and add the drained chickpeas and pulse a few times
to incorporate into a fine paste. The consistency of the paste should be
grainy with a shade of pistachio green. Taste and adjust the seasoning, if
needed, then add the baking soda. Add the flour if you think the mixture
needs help with binding. Mix well to combine.

3 Using a greased tablespoon, form the chickpea mixture into 1-inch
patties, handling the mixture as little as possible. You should make
20 to 24 patties. Place on a cookie sheet and set aside to become firm.

4 Heat the oven to low. Pour the oil into a wide, deep saucepan
or wok and place over medium heat. Alternatively, use a deep-fat fryer,
in which case you'll need more oil. The oil is ready when it begins
to bubble or reaches 350°F. If you don't have a thermometer, check the
readiness of the oil by dropping a small piece of the falafel mixture into
the oil: if it browns within 1 minute, the oil is ready.

5 Gently transfer the patties into the hot oil in 2 or 3 batches and fry
1 to 2 minutes on each side until golden brown (or 3 to 4 minutes
in total if deep-frying). Using a slotted spoon, transfer the patties
to a plate lined with paper towels. Place in the oven while deep-frying
the remaining patties. Once cooked, cut the patties in half, if you like.
Add the Arabic bread to the oven and warm 1 minute.

6 Lay a loaf of bread on a plate. Sprinkle lettuce in the center of the
loaf. Put some of the falafel patties on top, drizzle with tarator, top with
accompaniments and sprinkle with parsley. Tightly roll up the bread,
tucking in one end. Repeat with the remaining ingredients. Serve with
napkins to soak up the juices.

Sabich Salad

SERVES 4
PREPARATION TIME: 15 minutes,
  plus making the bread and
  hummus
COOKING TIME: 20 minutes

8 eggs

2 Earl Grey tea bags

skins of 2 small yellow onions

1 to 2 teaspoons sea salt, plus extra
  for seasoning

2 eggplants, sliced lengthwise into
  ½-inch-thick slices

5 tablespoons olive oil

4 tablespoons tahini

1 garlic clove, finely chopped
  or crushed

a pinch dried chili flakes

juice of 1½ lemons

4 loaves Arabic Bread, unpeeled
  (see page 217)

1 small cucumber, finely chopped

1 small red onion, finely chopped

1 tomato, finely chopped

4 tablespoons Hummus (see
  page 27)

chopped parsley and cilantro leaves,
  to sprinkle

freshly ground black pepper

Green Mango Chutney (see page
  143), to serve

This rowdy salad is based on the sabich sandwich, a very popular breakfast fare in and around Jerusalem. The eggs are traditionally boiled gently for 6 hours over very low heat. In an effort to remain sane, however, I prefer to bring them to the boiling point, then remove them from the heat and leave them to wait in the hot water while I prepare the salad.

1 Heat the broiler to high. Put the eggs, tea bags, onion skins and salt in a saucepan and cover with water. Bring to a boil, then remove from the heat and leave to sit while you prepare the rest of the salad.

2 Brush the eggplant slices with 1½ teaspoons of the oil on each side, then season with salt and pepper on both sides.

3 Place a griddle pan over high heat until h___ ther cook the eggplant 2 to 3 minutes on each side until soft and cooked th ough, with grill marks. You might need to do this in several batches.

4 Put the tahini in a mixing bowl, add the garlic, chili flakes, juice of 1 lemon and 3 tablespoons water and mix well. Season with salt and pepper and set aside.

5 Toast the bread under the hot broiler about 2 minutes on each side until crisp and golden brown.

6 Meanwhile, to make the salsa, put the cucumber, red onion and tomato in a serving bowl and mix well. Drizzle the remaining ___ a squeeze of lemon juice over. Season to taste with salt and pepper.

7 Before serving, run the eggs under cold water for just long enough so you can handle them, then peel the eggs and slice thinly.

8 Place the crisp Arabic Bread rounds on four plates. Spread each with hummus, then add a few eggplant slices and some egg slices. Drizzle the tomato and cucumber salsa and some of the tahini dressing over. Sprinkle with the herbs and serve with a dollop of Green Mango Chutney.

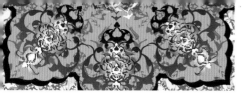

koshari

SERVES 4
PREPARATION TIME: 25 minutes
COOKING TIME: 30 minutes

5 tablespoons olive oil

2 small, mild red chilies (or more to taste), seeded and finely chopped

6 garlic cloves, finely chopped

1 teaspoon ground cumin

2¼ cups finely chopped tomatoes, or 1 can (15-oz.) crushed tomatoes

¾ cup brown lentils, rinsed

3 tablespoons sunflower oil

2½ cups thinly sliced onions

5 ounces spaghetti, tagliatelle or reshteh

1 cup elbow macaroni

1 heaped cup coarse or extra coarse bulgur wheat (grade 3 or 4)

4 teaspoons salted butter

½ cup vermicelli broken into ½-inch pieces (or bought already broken from a Middle Eastern grocery store)

mint leaves, to sprinkle

sea salt and freshly ground black pepper

Undressed Herb Salad (see page 67), to serve

lime wedges, to serve

While koshari might be Egypt's glorious answer to street food, the word is not Arabic, but rather derived from the Hindi word khichri, meaning a dish of rice and lentils. It's an import, brought to Egypt by the British Army.

1 Heat 2 tablespoons of the olive oil in a heavy-bottomed saucepan over medium heat. Add the chilies, garlic and cumin and cook about 1 minute until aromatic. Add the tomatoes and bring to a boil, then reduce the heat to low and leave to simmer, uncovered, 20 minutes, stirring often, until the mixture is thick and saucelike. Season to taste with salt and pepper.

2 At the same time, heat a heavy-bottomed saucepan of water over high heat and add the lentils. Bring to a boil, then reduce the heat to low, cover and simmer 20 to 30 minutes until soft. Drain, then cover to keep warm.

3 Meanwhile, heat the sunflower oil in a skillet over medium heat. Add the onions and fry about 15 minutes, stirring often, until caramelized and golden brown. Transfer to a plate lined with paper towels. Set the empty pan to one side.

4 Heat another large saucepan of water over high heat, season with salt and add another tablespoon of olive oil. Bring to a boil, then add the spaghetti and macaroni at the same time and cook 10 minutes, or according to the package directions. The macaroni might take a bit longer to cook, in which case add it first and adjust the timing.

5 Put the bulgur in a small heatproof bowl, cover with double its volume of boiling water and leave to soak until all the water is absorbed and the bulgur is tender, about 10 to 15 minutes.

6 Heat the skillet used for the onions over medium heat. Add the butter and fry the vermicelli 3 to 5 minutes until golden and crisp, stirring often. Transfer to a plate lined with paper towels and set aside.

7 When the pasta finishes cooking, drain it well, then return it to the pan and toss with the remaining olive oil. Cover and keep warm.

8 Place a layer of pasta on each of four plates, sprinkle the bulgur over, then add the vermicelli, lentils and tomato sauce. Sprinkle with the caramelized onions and mint. Serve with an Undressed Herb Salad and lime wedges for squeezing over.

upSide-down cauLifLower rice caKe

SERVES 4
PREPARATION TIME: 30 minutes,
 plus making the rice, harissa and
 stock, and resting
COOKING TIME: 1 hour 5 minutes

2 cups rice, soaked (see steps 1 and
 2 of Parboiled Rice, page 214)

1 garlic bulb, cloves separated and
 finely chopped

1 cardamom pod, crushed

¼ teaspoon ground cinnamon

¼ teaspoon ground allspice

½ teaspoon dried lime powder

½ teaspoon Harissa (see page 210)

3½ cups Vegetable Stock (see
 page 211)

7 tablespoons olive oil

2 small red onions

1½ cups parsnips thinly sliced
 lengthwise

2¾ cups cauliflower florets

14 ounces eggplant, partially
 peeled lengthwise to leave strips
 of peel about 1 inch wide, then cut
 lengthwise into ¾-inch slices

⅓ cup canned chestnuts, drained
 and thinly sliced, or 2½ ounces
 cooked fresh chestnuts

⅔ cup cherry tomatoes,
 thinly sliced

butter, for greasing

¼ cup blanched almonds

2 tablespoons pine nuts

mint leaves, to sprinkle

pomegranate seeds (see page 216),
 to sprinkle

sea salt

Greek yogurt, to serve

The Arabic title of this Jordanian-Palestinian dish literally means "flipped over." While the traditional version includes meat, I have opted to keep it vegetarian. Although it's traditionally served warm, I like it better cold. Adjust the harissa to taste.

1 Put the soaked rice in a heavy-bottomed saucepan over medium heat. Add the garlic, cardamom, cinnamon, allspice, dried lime powder, harissa and vegetable stock. Cover and bring to a boil, then reduce the heat and simmer 15 minutes, or until the liquid is absorbed. The rice will still have a little bite to it, but will steam more in the oven later in the recipe.

2 Heat the oven to 400°F. Put 2 tablespoons of the oil in a deep skillet over medium heat. Fry the onions about 5 minutes until they are translucent and slightly golden. Transfer to a plate lined with paper towels and set aside.

3 Put the parsnips in a thin layer on a baking sheet and brush both sides with some of the oil. Put the cauliflower on another baking sheet and toss with a little oil. Repeat with the eggplant.

4 Bake the vegetables in the oven until the parsnips are just tender, about 10 minutes; the cauliflower is tender but still with a little bite, about 15 minutes; and the eggplant is golden and pliable, 10 to 15 minutes. Alternatively, you can fry all these vegetables: start by frying the parsnips 3 to 4 minutes until golden and crisp. Repeat with the cauliflower, frying about 3 minutes until golden, then fry the eggplant about 4 minutes, first sprinkling the slices with salt.

5 Reduce the oven temperature to 350°F. Grease a Bundt pan and line the bottom and side with eggplant slices, with the wide ends at the bottom, and then the parsnips with the wide ends at the top (laid in opposite directions to create a full layer of vegetables). Layer in one-third of the rice, half the cauliflower, half the red onions, half the chestnuts and half the tomato slices. Repeat and finish off with a layer of rice, pressing down gently. Cover very tightly with foil and bake in the oven 30 minutes, or until the rice is tender. Remove from the oven and leave to rest 20 minutes before gently inverting the cake onto a serving plate. If it falls apart a bit, gently reconstruct it.

6 Toast the almonds and pine nuts in a heavy-bottomed pan over medium heat 1 to 2 minutes until golden and fragrant, shaking the pan often. Sprinkle the toasted nuts, mint and pomegranate seeds over the rice cake and serve hot or cold with yogurt on the side.

Zucchini Stuffed With Herbed Rice

SERVES 4
PREPARATION TIME: 1 hour
COOKING TIME: 1 hour 10 minutes

2 ¼ pounds zucchini

1 pound 6 ounces tomatoes

2 small onions

½ cup short-grain rice

½ teaspoon ground allspice

1 handful parsley leaves,
    finely chopped

3 tablespoons finely chopped
    mint leaves

4 tablespoons olive oil

juice of 2 lemons

1 tablespoon pine nuts

1 heaped tablespoon tomato paste

5 garlic cloves

sea salt and freshly ground black
    pepper

Greek yogurt, to serve

warm Arabic Bread (see page 217),
    to serve

Reserve the zucchini cores to make succulent fritters (see page 50). The stuffing is essentially a tabbouleh mixture combined with rice—it's a great way to use up leftover tabbouleh.

1 Rinse the zucchini and trim off the stem ends. Using a vegetable corer, scrape out the flesh and seeds, being sure to remove as much of it as you can without breaking through the zucchini skin. If you do accidentally cut too hard and crack a zucchini, you can still stuff it but you will need to be gentle with it. Set the hollowed-out zucchini aside.

2 Finely chop one of the tomatoes and one of the onions and put them in a mixing bowl. Add the rice, half the allspice, the parsley, 1 tablespoon of the mint, half the oil and half the lemon juice. Mix well and season to taste with salt and pepper. Toast the pine nuts in a heavy-bottomed pan over medium heat 1 to 2 minutes until golden and fragrant, shaking the pan often. Add them to the mixture.

3 Thinly slice the remaining tomatoes and onion. Drizzle the remaining oil in a heavy-bottomed flameproof dish or deep skillet, then arrange layers of tomato and onion rings over the bottom. Add the remaining allspice and some salt.

4 Stuff the zucchini by gently packing enough of the rice mixture to fill them three-quarters full, leaving room for the rice to expand. Put the stuffed zucchini on top of the tomato and onion layers in the pan.

5 Mix the tomato paste with 1 cup plus 2 tablespoons water and pour the mixture over the stuffed zucchini. Season to taste with salt and pepper. Gently lay a heatproof plate that fits inside the dish on top of the zucchini to keep them compressed and minimizes any movement. Pour in enough additional water so the zucchini are immersed, though not necessarily the plate.

6 Place the dish over high heat and bring to a boil, then reduce the heat to medium-low and leave to simmer, covered, 45 to 60 minutes until the zucchini are tender. To check if they are ready, pierce gently with a fork: the flesh should be soft and the rice cooked.

7 Meanwhile, grind the garlic and a pinch salt using a mortar and pestle to make a paste. Add the remaining mint and pound another minute, then mix in the remaining lemon juice. Drizzle the garlic and lemon mixture over the zucchini. Leave to simmer 5 minutes longer so the flavors seep in. Serve warm or at room temperature with yogurt and warm Arabic Bread.

grape leaves with bulgur, figs and nuts

SERVES 4
PREPARATION TIME: 1 hour,
  plus resting
COOKING TIME: 1 hour 40 minutes
  to 2 hours 10 minutes

24 packaged grape leaves,
  or 24 fresh grape leaves

juice of 2 lemons

⅔ cup olive oil

1 small red onion, thinly sliced

2 garlic cloves, finely chopped

½ cup coarse bulgur wheat (grade
  3), short-grain rice or risotto rice

2 ripe fresh figs or 2 ready-to-eat
  dried figs, finely chopped

¼ cup walnut halves, finely
  chopped

2 tablespoons finely chopped
  parsley leaves

2 tablespoons finely chopped mint
  leaves

2 tablespoons finely chopped
  cilantro leaves

1 teaspoon ground allspice

1 teaspoon Aleppo pepper flakes or
  crushed chili flakes

1 large tomato, cut into ½-inch
  slices

1 onion, cut into ½-inch slices

1 potato, cut into ½-inch slices

sea salt and freshly ground black
  pepper

Greek yogurt, to serve

Usually known by their Turkish name "dolma," which means "to be stuffed," the word encompasses a whole family of stuffed vegetables. To create a hearty main course, add a layer of lamb chops between the tomatoes and potatoes.

1 If using packaged grape leaves, fill a bowl with warm water. Remove the grape leaves from the packaging or brine and separate the leaves, one by one, transferring them to a bowl of water. Leave to soak about 10 minutes. Change the water and soak the leaves again.

2 If using fresh grape leaves, pour boiling water into a heatproof bowl, add the juice of half a lemon, then immerse the fresh grape leaves in the boiling water 3 to 4 minutes until soft. Drain, then rinse under cold water and shake off the excess water. Put the leaves on a cutting board. Cut the hard stems out and discard; set aside the leaves.

3 Heat 2 tablespoons of the oil in a heavy-bottomed skillet over medium heat. Add the onion and fry 4 to 5 minutes until softened. Add the garlic and fry 1 minute until aromatic, stirring often, then mix in the bulgur wheat, figs, walnuts, herbs, spices and 2 more tablespoons of the oil. Season to taste with salt and pepper and set aside.

4 Lightly grease a deep, heavy-bottomed saucepan with another 2 tablespoons of the oil and lay the tomato slices over the bottom, followed by onion slices and then potato slices. Sprinkle with salt.

5 Working with one grape leaf at a time, place it on the countertop, wide end facing you with the shiny side down and the protruding stem exposed. Place 1 teaspoon of the stuffing ½ inch from the bottom. Fold over the leaf and then the sides and begin rolling it into a tight cylindrical shape, seam-side down. Repeat with the remaining grape leaves and stuffing, layering the leaves over the potato layer as you finish rolling them. Make sure the grape leaves fit snugly inside the pan, then cover with water and weigh them down with a heatproof plate.

6 Cover the pan with a tight-fitting lid and bring to a boil. Reduce the heat to low and simmer 1½ to 2 hours until the grape leaves are meltingly smooth and the sauce is thick. If too much water evaporates and the grape leaves seem tough, add a little more water and continue cooking. When cooked, pour the remaining oil and lemon juice over and leave to stand 10 to 15 minutes before serving warm or cool, with yogurt.

fava beans with yogurt tahdeeg

SERVES 4
PREPARATION TIME: 45 minutes,
   plus making the rice and advieh
COOKING TIME: 50 minutes

1 ¾ pounds fresh fava beans
   in the pod, or 14 ounces frozen
   shelled fava beans

6 tablespoons sunflower oil

1 recipe quantity Parboiled Rice
   (see pages 214)

3 tablespoons Greek yogurt, plus
   extra to serve

1 teaspoon orange blossom water

1 handful dill leaves, finely chopped,
   plus extra for sprinkling

1 teaspoon Advieh 1 (see page 211)

zest and juice of 1 orange

6 garlic cloves, crushed

4 tablespoons unsalted butter

sea salt and freshly ground black
   pepper

This is a vibrant vegetarian rice dish that can be made with either fresh or frozen fava beans.

1 Shell the fresh fava beans, if using, then blanch and skin them as follows: Put the beans in a saucepan of boiling water and leave to boil for a maximum of 2 minutes. Drain, then transfer the beans to a bowl of ice water to stop them cooking. Slip the skins off. If using frozen beans, thaw them, then slip them out of their thick outer skins.

2 Pour the oil into a heavy-bottomed saucepan and heat over medium heat until the oil is sizzling.

3 Put 4 to 5 tablespoons of the rice in a bowl with the yogurt and orange blossom water and mix well. Spread it gently across the bottom of the saucepan to cover. This will form the tahdeeg.

4 Mix the remaining rice with the fava beans, dill, advieh, orange zest and juice and garlic and season to taste with salt and pepper. Sprinkle the rice lightly into the saucepan, building the mixture up into a dome shape. Using the handle of a wooden spoon, make three holes down into the rice, being careful not to puncture the tahdeeg.

5 Melt the butter in a small saucepan over low heat. Add 2 tablespoons water and mix well, then pour the mixture over the rice.

6 Wrap the saucepan lid in a clean dish towel and tie it into a tight knot at the handle, then use it to cover the pan as tightly as you can so steam does not escape. (The dish towel will prevent the moisture from dripping into the rice, making it soggy.)

7 Cook the rice over medium heat 2 to 3 minutes until the rice is steaming (you will see puffs of steam escaping at the edges of the lid), then reduce the heat to low and cook about 45 minutes, with the lid on all the time. Serve the rice and tahdeeg following the directions in steps 5–7 of Steamed Rice on page 214. Sprinkle the rice with dill and serve with extra yogurt.

mixed bean & herb noodle soup

SERVES 4
PREPARATION TIME: 30 minutes
   plus overnight soaking and
   making the stock
COOKING TIME: 1 hour 40 minutes,
   plus cooking the kidney beans
   (optional) and chickpeas until
   tender

4 tablespoons sunflower oil

3 large onions, thinly sliced

½ teaspoon turmeric

½ cup dried kidney beans, soaked overnight and cooked until tender (following the directions for chickpeas on page 215), or ½ can (15-oz.) kidney beans, drained and rinsed

¼ cup dried chickpeas, soaked overnight with 1 teaspoon baking soda added to the water, then cooked until tender (see page 215), drained

6½ cups Vegetable Stock (see page 211)

¼ cup brown lentils, rinsed

2 ounces reshteh or thin egg noodles

1 small handful finely chopped dill leaves

1 small handful finely chopped parsley leaves

1 small handful finely chopped cilantro leaves

3 ounces spinach leaves

juice of 1 lemon

sea salt and freshly ground pepper

TO SERVE
½ cup sour cream or liquid kashk

Mint & Butter Drizzle (see page 220)

warm Thin Flatbread (optional, see page 218)

lemon wedges (optional)

This hearty soup is a quintessential part of the Norouz (Persian New Year). The fine noodles, or reshteh, are associated with new beginnings and good fortune. You can substitute the reshteh with linguini, thin egg noodles or angel hair pasta broken into short pieces. If you use canned kidney beans, they should be added at the same time as the lentils.

1 Heat half the oil in a large, heavy-bottomed saucepan over low heat. Add one of the onions and cook 3 to 5 minutes until soft and translucent. Stir in the turmeric and fry for another 1 minute.

2 Add the kidney beans and chickpeas to the onion and pour in the stock. Increase the heat to high and bring to a boil, then lower the heat to medium-low and simmer 1 hour, or until the beans are tender.

3 Add the lentils to the pan and simmer 30 minutes longer, or until soft and tender, adding some water if the lentils are too dry.

4 Meanwhile, heat the remaining oil in a heavy-bottomed skillet over medium heat and fry the remaining onions until crisp and golden.

5 Add the reshteh, herbs, spinach and lemon juice to the beans and cook about 5 minutes until the noodles are cooked but still have a little bite to them and the spinach wilts. Season to taste with salt and pepper.

6 Sprinkle the golden onions over the top of the soup and serve with sour cream, Mint and Butter Drizzle, Thin Flatbreads and lemon wedges, if you want.

fava beans, peas & fennel tagine

SERVES 4
PREPARATION TIME: 15 minutes,
  plus making the lemon and stock
COOKING TIME: 40 minutes

4 teaspoons salted butter

1 leek, thinly sliced

5 garlic cloves, finely chopped

1 wedge Preserved Lemon (see
  page 212), peel rinsed and finely
  chopped

2-inch piece gingerroot, peeled and
  finely chopped

1 cup dry, citrusy white wine

14 ounces fennel bulbs, cut into
  8 wedges

4 artichoke hearts in brine, drained
  and quartered

1 handful shelled fava beans,
  skins removed

2 tablespoons finely chopped
  tarragon leaves

2¼ cups Vegetable Stock (see
  page 211)

a pinch ground saffron (see page
  212) or turmeric

1 handful shelled peas

4 ounces goat cheese, crumbled

sea salt and freshly ground black
  pepper

Couscous (see page 216), to serve

This is a really simple, but flavorsome, light and brothy stew that makes use of splendid spring vegetables. It's worked well to convert a few fennel-haters from the dark side. It's rustic in nature, so adjust the size of the vegetables, making them smaller, if you like.

1 Melt the butter in a heavy-bottomed pan over medium heat. Add the leek, cover and sweat 1 to 2 minutes until the are just beginning to become soft. Add the garlic, half the preserved lemon and the ginger, then cover and cook 1 minute, or until the mixture is aromatic.

2 Pour in the wine and bubble 4 to 5 minutes until it reduces by half. Add the fennel, artichoke hearts, fava beans and half the tarragon and toss well.

3 Meanwhile, heat the stock in a saucepan over medium heat, then add the saffron and pour the mixture over the vegetables. Cover and bring to a boil, then reduce the heat to low and simmer 20 to 25 minutes until the vegetables are cooked through.

4 Add the peas, the remaining tarragon and the remaining preserved lemon, season to taste with salt and pepper and simmer 5 minutes longer. Transfer to bowls, crumble over some goat cheese, if using, and serve with Couscous.

SLOW-COOKed fava bean & tomato stew

SERVES 4
PREPARATION TIME: 30 minutes,
  plus soaking and making the onion
  (optional)
COOKING TIME: 10 minutes

2 cups dried fava beans, soaked
  48 hours and cooked about 3 hours
  until soft, following the directions
  for cooking chickpeas on page 215

1 onion, trimmed and quartered
  (optional)

2 teaspoons salted butter

5 garlic cloves, finely chopped

2 tomatoes, finely chopped

4 tablespoons finely chopped
  cilantro leaves

1 tablespoon tahini

2 teaspoons ground cumin

juice of 2 lemons

4 tablespoons olive oil

sea salt and freshly ground black
  pepper

warm Arabic Bread (see page 217),
  to serve

4 hard-boiled eggs, halved, to serve
  (optional)

This wonderfully wholesome, cheap and filling stew is a staple of the Egyptian diet, where it's regularly enjoyed for breakfast topped with hard-boiled eggs. (See Sabich Salad on page 152 for another way of preparing the eggs.) The Arabic name for this dish is fool mudammas—the word mudammas originates from the Coptic word for "buried," and was probably applied to this dish following the ancient cooking method of burying a covered pot filled with beans and water under hot coals. Dried fava beans, which are brown in color, are very easy to find at Middle Eastern grocery stores.

1 Strain the cooked fava beans, reserving the cooking liquid.

2 Soak the onion quarters, if using, in a bowl of ice water 30 minutes to make the flavor milder and to keep the onion crisp.

3 Melt the butter in the empty pan from the fava beans over medium heat, then add the garlic and cook 1 minute, or until aromatic. Add the tomatoes and half the cilantro and cook 2 minutes longer.

4 Add the fava beans, ½ cup of the reserved cooking liquid, the tahini, 1½ teaspoons of the cumin, the lemon juice (it's best to taste the mixture as you add this to make sure it isn't too sour) and half the oil to the tomato mixture, then heat through. Season to taste with salt and pepper and stir well to combine. If the fava beans are still very firm, move some into a bowl, mash them with a potato masher and then return them to the pan.

5 Transfer the stew to a large serving dish, drizzle with the remaining oil and sprinkle the remaining cumin and cilantro over the top. Serve with Arabic Bread and with the onion and hard-boiled eggs, if you like.

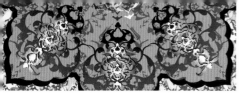

smoky eggplant & split pea stew

2 tablespoons sunflower oil

1 large onion, thinly sliced

1 ¼ cups yellow or green split peas

1 teaspoon Advieh 1 (see page 211)

3 garlic cloves, crushed

1 tomato, roughly chopped

4 tablespoons tomato paste

2 or 3 whole dried black limes (limu amani), pierced with the tip of a knife

1 tablespoon pomegranate molasses

4 cups eggplants cut into ¾-inch slices

4 tablespoons olive oil, or to taste

sea salt and freshly ground black pepper

TO SERVE
Chelow Rice (optional, see page 214)

Potato Matchsticks (see page 218)

Greek yogurt

Gheimeh is traditionally a lamb stew served with fried potatoes or eggplants, but I prefer this vegetarian version. Here, I have added chargrilled eggplant for an extra layer of smokiness. I serve this comforting stew with potato matchsticks rather than chunky fries.

1 Heat the sunflower oil in a large, shallow saucepan over medium-low heat. Add the onion and fry until light golden.

2 Rinse the split peas and add them to the pan with the advieh, garlic and tomato. Cover with about 4 cups water and mix well, then bring the mixture to a boil. Reduce the heat to low and simmer 15 minutes. Add the tomato paste and dried limes and cook 15 minutes longer, or until the split peas are cooked but still have a little bite to them.

3 Add a little more water, if needed, keeping in mind that the stew is meant to be thick, then simmer 30 minutes longer. Season with pomegranate molasses and salt and pepper.

4 Meanwhile, heat the broiler to medium-high or heat a griddle pan over medium-high heat. Rub the eggplant slices with salt and the olive oil, then broil or griddle about 10 minutes, turning occasionally, until soft and light brown.

5 Add the eggplant slices to the stew in one or two layers, pushing them down gently so they are just covered with the stew juices, then cover and simmer 20 minutes longer. The eggplant should have a melt-in-your-mouth texture, while the split peas should be tender but not disintegrating. Serve the stew with the Chelow Rice, if you like, and Potato Matchsticks, with yogurt on the side.

Note: You will need only half a batch of the Potato Matchsticks if serving the stew with the rice, too.

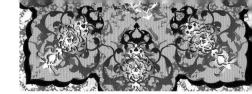

mess of pottage

SERVES 4
PREPARATION TIME: 20 minutes
COOKING TIME: 1 hour 20 minutes

1½ cups brown lentils, picked of any impurities and rinsed

4 tablespoons sunflower oil

1 onion, finely chopped

2 tablespoons coarse bulgur wheat (grade 3), rinsed

1 teaspoon ground allspice

2 red onions, sliced into thin rings

2 tablespoons olive oil

sea salt

White Cabbage Salad (see page 220), to serve

warm Arabic Bread (see page 217), to serve

These days, mujadarah holds a very special place in my heart. Just as Esau, according to the Book of Genesis, traded his birthright away to his brother Jacob for what many believe to have been a form of this "Mess of Pottage", when I'm stressed and missing home there's not much I wouldn't give up for a comforting bowl of this warming lentil stew.

1 Put the lentils in a heavy-bottomed saucepan, cover with about 4 cups water and bring to a boil over medium-high heat. Reduce the heat to low and simmer about 1 hour until the lentils are soft.

2 Meanwhile, heat half the sunflower oil in a skillet over medium heat. Add the onion and fry about 5 minutes until soft and light golden.

3 Use a slotted spoon to remove the onions from the pan and add them to the cooked lentil mixture. Add 1 cup plus 2 tablespoons water, the bulgur and allspice. Season to taste with salt and simmer 20 minutes longer.

4 Meanwhile, heat the remaining sunflower oil in the skillet over medium heat and fry the red onion rings 10 to 15 minutes until soft and lightly colored. Remove the pan from the heat and transfer the onions to a plate lined with paper towels, using a slotted spoon.

5 Once the lentil mixture is cooked (the consistency should be like thick, moist oatmeal), pour in the olive oil and mix well. Adjust the seasoning, if required, then transfer to a large serving dish or individual bowls and leave to cool to room temperature. Top with the caramelized red onion rings and serve with a White Cabbage Salad and Arabic Bread.

teta's smoky musaqa'a

SERVES 4
PREPARATION TIME: 30 minutes,
  plus soaking the chickpeas
  (optional)
COOKING TIME: 1 hour 5 minutes,
  plus cooking the chickpeas until
  they are just tender (optional)

2¼ pounds eggplants

½ cup olive oil

2¼ pounds beefsteak tomatoes

2 tablespoons sunflower oil

1 onion, thinly sliced into rings

3 garlic cloves, crushed with the
  blade of a knife

heaped ½ cup dried chickpeas,
  soaked overnight and cooked until
  tender (see page 215), or ½ can
  (15-oz.) chickpeas, drained and
  rinsed

½ teaspoon ground allspice

1 tablespoon tomato paste (optional)

sea salt and freshly ground black
  pepper

TO SERVE
Greek yogurt

mint leaves (optional)

Arabic Bread (optional, see page
  217)

Vermicelli Rice (optional, see page
  215)

*The word moussaka, applied to the famous Greek dish, doesn't
actually have any meaning in the Greek language. Instead, it's
thought the dish came to Greece by way of the Phoenicians and
then took on French influences (hence the béchamel sauce).
Meaning "cold" or "chilled" in Arabic, musaqa'a is a humble
vegetarian stew that is best served at room temperature.*

1 Heat the oven to 400°F. Partially skin the eggplants, leaving strips
of skin about 1 inch wide, then cut them lengthwise into ¾-inch-thick
slices. Brush the slices on both sides with 6 tablespoons of the olive oil
(or more or less, as preferred) and place in an 8- x 6-inch baking dish,
overlapping, as necessary. Sprinkle with a little salt and bake in the
oven about 20 minutes until soft.

2 Alternatively, heat the broiler to medium-high and broil the prepared
eggplant slices about 5 minutes on each side until soft and lightly
colored. Transfer to a plate and set aside.

3 Core the tomatoes and score the bottoms with a sharp knife. Put them
in a heatproof bowl. Pour enough boiling water to cover over and leave
1 minute or until the skins begin to peel. Drain the tomatoes and plunge
them into cold water to stop them cooking, then peel off the skins and
discard. Cut the tomatoes in half, scoop out and discard the seeds, then
slice the flesh into ¼-inch-thick slices.

4 Heat the sunflower oil in a heavy-bottomed saucepan over medium
heat. Add the onion and garlic, then cover and sweat 4 to 5 minutes,
stirring often, until translucent. Add the tomato slices and chickpeas
in layers, seasoning each layer with a pinch of allspice and salt and
pepper. Cover with about 1 cup water. If the tomatoes are not a rich red
colour, then add the tomato paste for more depth of flavor and color.
Cover the pan and bring to a boil, then reduce the heat to low and leave
to simmer 20 minutes.

5 Add the cooked eggplant slices on top of the stew in layers,
overlapping if necessary. Gently press them down just enough so they
are lightly covered by the tomato broth. Cover and cook 20 minutes
longer. Remove the pan from the heat, uncover and leave to cool
down to room temperature. Serve with the yogurt and with mint for
sprinkling, Arabic Bread and Vermicelli Rice, if you like.

desserts

semolina pancakes

SERVES 4
PREPARATION TIME: 25 minutes,
 plus rising
COOKING TIME: about 30 minutes

½ cup milk

1 teaspoon active dry yeast

¼ teaspoon sugar

⅔ cup semolina flour (also known as
fine semolina)

½ cup plus 1 tablespoon
self-rising flour

1 teaspoon baking powder

a pinch fine sea salt

¾ cup blanched almonds

4 tablespoons argan oil

2 tablespoons honey

1 cup plus 2 tablespoons ricotta
or 1 recipe quantity Lebanese
Clotted Cream (see page 215)

2 tablespoons roughly chopped
honeycomb

*These semolina pancakes are known as beghrir, which means
"1,000 holes." The name refers to the multitude of holes that
develop on the surface as they cook.*

1 Warm the milk in a saucepan over low heat. Mix the yeast and sugar
with 3 tablespoons of the warmed milk, then pour this mixture into
a large mixing bowl and set aside. Reserve the remaining warm milk.

2 Sift the semolina, flour, the baking powder and salt into a large
mixing bowl.

3 Add the remaining milk to the yeast mixture along with ½ cup
warm water and whisk well. Add the dry ingredients a little at a time,
whisking vigorously until they are well incorporated and the mixture
is smooth.

4 Cover the bowl with a dish towel and set aside in a warm place
at least 1 hour until the mixture is frothy and doubles in size. If you are
not making the pancakes until the next day, leave the mixture covered
overnight in the refrigerator as it rises.

5 Meanwhile, heat the oven 300°F. Spread the almonds on a baking
sheet and toast 5 to 7 minutes until golden, shaking the pan to toss
them around halfway through the cooking time. Transfer to a mortar
and pestle or a small blender and grind about 5 minutes until you get
a very smooth, wet paste, stopping to scrape down the side every once
in a while. Transfer the paste to a serving bowl and mix in the argan oil
and honey. Taste and add more oil and/or honey, if you like. Leave the
oven on.

6 When you're ready to cook the pancakes, whisk the batter again.
It should be the texture of heavy cream (thin with a little water, if
necessary). Place a nonstick pan over medium-low heat. Working in
batches, pour 1 tablespoon of the batter into the pan to create a thin,
round pancake, about 3 inches in diameter, tilting the pan if necessary,
then repeat, spacing the pancakes slightly apart. Cook on one side 1
to 2 minutes until plenty of holes develop, the tops have set and the
bottoms are golden. Stack the first batch of pancakes between sheets of
parchment paper on an ovenproof plate and keep warm in the oven.
Repeat with the remaining batter to make about 24 pancakes in total.

7 To create half-moon shapes, seal the edges of the pancakes together
by pinching them together only halfway along. Spoon a little ricotta into
each pancake, then drizzle the almond butter over the top. Sprinkle with
honeycomb and serve.

fruit cocktail with clotted cream & nuts

SERVES 4
PREPARATION TIME: 15 minutes,
  plus making the clotted cream

8 strawberries

1 small pineapple

1 avocado

2 kiwifruit

1 small mango

4 tablespoons shelled pistachios

1 cup banana and strawberry juice

1 recipe quantity Lebanese Clotted
  Cream (see page 215)

4 tablespoons blanched almonds,
  roughly chopped

4 tablespoons honey

Refreshingly satisfying fruit cocktail concoctions are popular across the Levant and are enjoyed throughout the day. They are a great way to make use of whatever seasonal fruits are available.

1 Prepare the fruits as necessary, then chop into cubes or pieces, depending on the fruits' shape, measuring roughly ¾ inch.

2 Put the pistachios in a heatproof bowl and pour boiling water over to cover. Leave 1 to 2 minutes to let the skins loosen. Strain the nuts, then rub them dry, in batches if needed, using a dish towel. Discard the loose skins and rinse the pistachios well under cold running water to remove any remaining skin. Dust off the skins from the dish towel used earlier and pat the pistachios dry once more. Roughly chop them.

3 Pour the banana and strawberry juice equally into four tall cocktail glasses, add the fruit in layers and then spoon the Lebanese Clotted Cream over. Sprinkle with the pistachios and almonds and drizzle with the honey. Serve immediately.

Lebanese Clotted Cream

with Dulche de Leche & Caramelized Bananas

SERVES 4
PREPARATION TIME: 5 minutes,
  plus cooling and making the
  clotted cream
COOKING TIME: 1 hour 5 minutes

1 ¼ cups sweetened condensed milk

1 or 2 pinches sea salt flakes, plus
  extra to serve

1 tablespoon butter

3 bananas, thinly sliced

2 tablespoons dark rum or
  pineapple juice

2 recipe quantities Lebanese Clotted
  Cream (see page 215)

Growing up, we lived on a dairy farm for a while, where we made our own clotted cream. This creamy treat, loosely based on a popular dessert known as layali Lubnan (or Lebanese nights), uses a version of clotted cream made by adding cornstarch, which is easier to prepare. If preferred, you can make the dulce de leche in advance and warm it through gently before using in the recipe (see step 5).

1 Heat the oven to 425°F. To make the dulche de leche, pour the sweetened condensed milk into a shallow baking dish and sprinkle a pinch of the sea salt flakes over. Stir well.

2 Cover the baking dish with foil and place it in a deep roasting pan. Pour enough hot water into the pan so it reaches halfway up the sides of the dish, creating a bain marie.

3 Place the bain marie and baking dish in the oven and bake about 1 hour until the mixture is caramelized and brown, checking occasionally to make sure it isn't burning and adding more hot water as necessary to keep the level constant. Remove the dish from the oven and set aside.

4 Melt the butter in a heavy-bottomed skillet over medium heat. Add the bananas and rum, if using. Flambé the ingredients a few seconds, if desired, or bubble 1 to 2 minutes until the alcohol reduces a little. Remove the pan from the heat and toss to combine so the banana slices are covered with the buttery juices.

5 If the dulce de leche has been resting in the refrigerator or has cooled, warm it gently by resting the bowl over a pan of hot water and stirring until it returns to a thick pouring consistency.

6 Divide the clotted cream among four serving bowls, add a drizzle of the dulce de leche and top with the caramelized banana slices. Sprinkle with more sea salt flakes, if you like, and serve.

pomegranate & rose quark summer cake

SERVES 8
PREPARATION TIME: 45 minutes,
 plus cooling and chilling
COOKING TIME: 45 minutes

5 eggs, at room temperature

1 cup superfine sugar

zest of ½ lemon

1 cup less 2 tablespoons self-rising
 flour

small piece cold unsalted butter

7 tablespoons whipping or heavy
 cream

8 gelatin leaves or 2 envelops
 unflavored powdered gelatin

2¼ cups quark

juice of 1 lemon

¼ teaspoon rosewater or vanilla
 extract (optional)

seeds from 1 pomegranate (see page
 216), plus extra to decorate

confectioners' sugar, to dust

chopped mint leaves, to sprinkle

It's a bold statement, but it's safe to say this marvelous cake falls into my "top-five favorite cakes" category. The following Middle Easternized version is based on my friend Sascha Minn's quark summer cake, rather than a classic dessert from the region. It's an elegant cake: summery, zesty, light and fluffy. The quark cheese keeps the fat content to a minimum, and Greek yogurt can be substituted if you're unable to find quark. If you're averse to raw eggs, you can omit them, although it will affect the filling's texture. Either way, wash a slice of this cake down with a glass of sparkling wine and forget your worries.

1 Separate two of the eggs; put the egg whites in a glass mixing bowl and the egg yolks into a large mixing bowl. (If you have time, chill the glass bowl first, because this will improve the texture of the egg whites.)

2 Whisk the egg whites vigorously 2 minutes until you achieve soft peaks, keeping the mixer or whisk moving around the edge and the middle at all times to make sure all the egg white is mixed thoroughly. Set aside.

3 Add a whole egg to the egg yolks in the large mixing bowl along with ½ cup of the sugar and 1 tablespoon water. Beat about 1 minute until you achieve a creamy consistency.

4 Add the lemon zest to the bowl, then sift in the flour and beat about 1 minute to incorporate. Next, add in the whisked egg whites and fold them in thoroughly with a large metal spoon, making sure to remove any lumps. Try not to tap the bowl with the spoon, because you'll lose the air, which will reduce the general fluffiness of the cake.

5 Heat the oven to 325°F. Put the butter in the middle of an 8-inch springform pan and line with parchment paper, cutting around the edge closely so it fits the bottom. (The butter will help the parchment paper to stick to the pan.) Pour the batter into the prepared pan and level the surface with the back of a spoon.

6 Bake the cake on the top shelf of the oven 35 to 40 minutes until it is light golden and a skewer inserted into the middle comes out clean.

7 Leave the cake to cool about 20 minutes before releasing the bottom and carefully peeling off the parchment paper. Using a serrated knife, carefully slice the cake horizontally into two layers, turning it as you go to help keep the knife level. Transfer the two cake layers to a wire rack to cool.

8 Put the cream in a bowl and whip about 2 minutes until soft peaks form. Be careful not to overwhip. Set aside.

9 Cut up the leaf gelatin, if using, into smaller pieces using kitchen scissors. Put the pieces in a small bowl, cover with cold water and leave to soak 2 minutes, then drain well. Return the gelatin to the bowl and pour 4 tablespoons hot water over as you whisk vigorously, making sure all the gelatin dissolves and there are not any lumps remaining. Alternatively, if using powdered gelatin, follow the package directions.

10 Separate the two remaining eggs. Whisk the egg whites as in step 2. Put the yolks and remaining sugar in a large mixing bowl and beat vigorously 1 to 2 minutes, then pour in the gelatin and continue beating vigorously.

11 Add the quark, whipped cream, lemon juice and rosewater, if using, and fold into the mixture with a large metal spoon. Add the whisked egg whites and gently fold them in, just enough to incorporate without any lumps. Add the pomegranate seeds and gently fold them in.

12 Place the cake pan, bottomed removed, on a serving plate. Add the bottom layer of the cake, cut-side up, and lock the pan. Pour in the filling, gently spread it level and then cover with the other cake layer. Transfer the pan to the refrigerator and leave the cake to chill at least 1 hour until the filling sets. Dust with confectioners' sugar and sprinkle with extra pomegranate seeds and mint, then serve.

evaporated milk pudding
with Crushed Arabic Coffee

SERVES 4
PREPARATION TIME: 10 minutes,
 plus cooling and setting
COOKING TIME: 15 minutes

¾ cup plus 2 tablespoons whole milk

¾ cup plus 2 tablespoon evaporated milk or unsweetened condensed milk

4 tablespoons sugar

3 tablespoons cornstarch

large pinch ground cardamom

few drops rosewater

1 tablespoon Arabic coffee, espresso beans or dark chocolate, finely chopped, to decorate

1 tablespoon shelled pistachios, finely chopped, to decorate

Based on the classic Middle Eastern milk flan known as muhallabiah, this dessert also draws inspiration from Arabic coffee. The milk mixture is infused with cardamom, a spice with which Arabic coffee is commonly brewed. The creamy sweetness is contrasted splendidly with the bitter coffee beans. It's an incredibly simple and rapid way to satiate a sweet craving with very minimal mess. Adjust the rosewater to taste. Note that evaporated milk is also sometimes known as unsweetened condensed milk. Be careful not to use sweetened condensed milk by mistake.

1 Put the milk, evaporated milk, sugar, cornstarch and cardamom into a heavy-bottomed pan and whisk well to combine. When the mixture is smooth, put the pan over medium-low heat and bring it to a boil, whisking continuously until thick, and making sure it does not boil over. Once the mixture coats the back of a spoon, remove the pan from the heat.

2 Pour the mixture through a fine strainer secured over a measuring jug. Add the rosewater and leave to cool slightly, 10 to 15 minutes.

3 Pour the mixture into glasses or dessert bowls, cover tightly with plastic wrap and place in the refrigerator about 2–3 hours until really cold and set.

4 When the puddings are cold and set, remove them from the refrigerator and sprinkle with Arabic coffee beans and pistachios, then serve.

Saffron Rice Pudding

SERVES 4

PREPARATION TIME: 15 minutes, plus making the saffron liquid and chilling

COOKING TIME: 1 hour 10 minutes

4 ready-to-eat dried figs

⅓ cup honey

1 tablespoon rosewater

4⅓ cups whole milk

2 tablespoons unsalted butter

1 teaspoon ground cardamom

1 teaspoon ground cinnamon, plus extra for sprinkling

1 teaspoon Saffron Liquid (see page 212)

½ cup short-grain rice

⅔ cup heavy cream

2 tablespoons slivered almonds, to sprinkle

Nearly every culture has an adaptation of this ancient rice dish. This delicate and creamy version is inspired by two different Persian rice puddings: shir berenj and shollehzard. The former has a topping of honey or jam; the latter incorporates saffron. In Iran, a person will serve this dish to give thanks for their good fortune or to honor the departed.

1 Heat the oven to 350°F. Slice the figs lengthwise into sixths and place in a baking dish.

2 Bake in the oven 10 to 15 minutes until tender. Meanwhile, mix 6 tablespoons of the honey with the rosewater. Remove the figs from the oven and pour the rose-and-honey mixture over them. Set aside to cool.

3 Put the milk, the remaining honey, the butter, cardamom, cinnamon and saffron liquid in a large, heavy-bottomed saucepan and bring the mixture to a boil. Meanwhile, rinse the rice several times under cold running water.

4 Stir the mixture well, then reduce the heat to low. Add the rice and bring just to a boil, then simmer 50 minutes longer, stirring occasionally, until the rice is very soft and begins to disintegrate. The mixture should thicken into a pudding. Remove the pan from the heat and set aside to cool.

5 Pour the cream into a bowl and whip until it forms stiff peaks. Gently fold it into the cool rice. Pour the pudding into four dishes and leave to cool, then cover with plastic wrap and put in the refrigerator to chill for several hours.

6 Meanwhile, toast the slivered almonds in a heavy-bottomed pan over medium heat 1 to 2 minutes until golden and fragrant, shaking the pan often.

7 Before serving, sprinkle each pudding with a pinch cinnamon, add the honeyed figs and sprinkle with the toasted almonds.

cardamom-scented profiteroles

MAKES ABOUT 10
PREPARATION TIME: 30 minutes,
 plus cooling
COOKING TIME: 30 minutes

½ cup milk

½ cup (1 stick) butter

1 cup all-purpose flour

a pinch salt

4 eggs

zest of 1 lime

1 teaspoon ground cardamom

2 cups heavy cream

½ cup sugar

2 tablespoons rosewater

½ cup shelled pistachios,
 finely chopped

4 tablespoons pomegranate
 molasses

confectioners' sugar, for dusting

dried edible rose petals, to decorate
 (optional)

*Profiteroles might look and sound daunting, but they are
actually super-easy to make and don't take that much time,
either. Here is my twist on Iran's popular cream-filled pastries.*

1 Heat the oven to 350°F. Line a large baking sheet with parchment
paper. To make the choux pastry dough, put the milk, butter and
½ cup water in a heavy-bottomed saucepan over medium heat until
the butter melts, then bring to a boil. Reduce the heat to low and add
the flour and salt, then beat vigorously with a wooden spoon until the
mixture forms a smooth paste and starts to pull away from the side
of the pan.

2 Remove the pan from the heat and leave the mixture to cool
2 to 3 minutes to prevent the eggs curdling. Beat in the eggs, one
at a time, making sure each is thoroughly incorporated before you add
the next. Continue beating until the mixture forms a smooth, thick paste.
Sprinkle half the lime zest and the cardamom over and gently stir until
just combined.

3 Spoon a heaped tablespoon of the choux pastry dough onto the
prepared baking sheet, sliding it off with your finger if needed. Repeat
with the rest of the mixture, leaving about 2 inches between each one
to allow for expansion during cooking, making about ten profiteroles.

4 Bake in the oven 20 to 25 minutes until the profiteroles are puffed
up and are golden brown. Turn off the oven, leaving the profiteroles
inside with the door slightly ajar for about 15 minutes. If you tap the
bottom of one of the profiteroles, it should make a hollow sound. Pierce
the side of each profiterole to release any hot air, which helps to prevent
them becoming soggy.

5 Put the cream and sugar in a mixing bowl and use an electric mixer
to beat the mixture until stiff peaks form. Add the rosewater, the
remaining lime zest and the pistachios and fold in gently. Put in the
refrigerator to firm up.

6 Once the profiteroles are cool, cut each one in half horizontally, but
not all the way through. Remove the chilled cream from the refrigerator
and use a toothpick to gently swirl in the pomegranate molasses.

7 Spoon 2 tablespoons of the cream into the cavity of each profiterole.
Dust with confectioners' sugar and decorate with rose petals, if you like.

tahini & chocolate brioche

SERVES 4
PREPARATION TIME: 45 minutes,
  plus rising
COOKING TIME: 50 minutes

4 tablespoons milk

1 envelope (¼-oz.) active dry yeast

2 cups all-purpose flour, plus extra
  for dusting

a pinch fine sea salt

3 tablespoons superfine sugar, plus
  an extra pinch

2 eggs plus 1 egg yolk

½ cup (1 stick) butter at room
  temperature, cut into cubes

1 teaspoon sunflower oil

1 tablespoon plus 2 teaspoons tahini

¼ cup chocolate chips

Armenian communities throughout the Middle East have contributed much to the cuisine across the region, and this brioche is inspired by their tahinov hatz, a type of sweet bread roll spread with sugar and cinnamon.

1 Warm the milk in a small saucepan until lukewarm. Sprinkle in the yeast and stir well.

2 Sift the flour and salt into a mixing bowl, add the sugar, yeasted milk mixture and both eggs and mix thoroughly by hand. Knead in the butter, one piece at a time. The result should be a soft and elastic dough with a sticky consistency.

3 Dust the countertop with flour. Lightly grease your hands with a few drops of the oil, then remove the dough from the bowl and shape it into a tight, smooth ball. Lightly grease the mixing bowl and return the dough ball to the bowl. Cover with a dish towel and leave in a warm place to rise 1 to 2 hours until it doubles in size.

4 Tip the dough out onto a lightly floured countertop and punch it down to deflate, then knead it 5 minutes, during which time it should become less sticky and more silky. Grease the bowl again and return the dough to the bowl. Cover and leave to rise in a warm place 1 hour longer, or until it doubles in size again.

5 Lightly dust the countertop with flour again. Remove the dough from the mixing bowl and cut it into eight even-size pieces, then roll each one into a ball. Working with one ball at time, and covering the others with a damp dish towel while you work, flatten each ball and brush each one with ½ teaspoon of the tahini, then sprinkle about one-eighth of the chocolate chips in the middle. Working with one ball at a time, gather the edges of the dough over the tahini and chocolate, pinching them together into pouches to seal in the filling tightly. Transfer to a nonstick 9- x 5-inch bread pan and repeat with the remaining balls. Cover and set aside 1 hour, or until they all double in size.

6 Shortly before the balls are fully risen, heat the oven to 350°F. In a bowl, whisk the egg yolk with 1 tablespoon water and the pinch of sugar to create an egg wash, then brush this over the top of the dough balls.

7 Bake in the oven 35 to 45 minutes until the top is golden brown and a skewer inserted into the middle comes out clean. Remove the brioche from the oven and leave it to stand 5 minutes before turning it out onto a wire rack to cool. When completely cool, cut into slices.

egyptian spiced bread pudding

SERVES 4
PREPARATION TIME: 15 minutes
COOKING TIME: 30 minutes

4 all-butter croissants

2 tablespoons raisins or dried mixed berries

2 tablespoons slivered almonds, plus extra to sprinkle

2 tablespoons pine nuts, plus extra for sprinkling

2 tablespoons roughly chopped shelled pistachios, plus extra for sprinkling

1 cup plus 2 tablespoons milk

5 tablespoons sugar

¼ teaspoon ground cinnamon

2 teaspoons orange blossom water

1 cup plus 2 tablespoons whipping cream

4 tablespoons shredded coconut

1 medium egg, beaten

This dessert, known as Um Ali Bread Pudding, is named after the mother um Ali. The tales of both the mother and the dessert are many and intriguing. This dessert is a quick and easy way to win legions of hearts. It's also a mouth-watering way to use up stale croissants—or a great reason to go and buy some!

1 Heat the oven to 350°F and line a baking sheet with parchment paper.

2 Tear the croissants into bite-size pieces, place them on the baking sheet and bake in the oven 10 minutes, or until crisp and golden.

3 Spread the croissant pieces across the bottom of an 11-inch square flameproof baking dish. Sprinkle the raisins, almonds, pine nuts and pistachios over, making sure they are distributed evenly.

4 Heat the milk in a heavy-bottomed saucepan over medium heat. Add 3 tablespoons of the sugar and mix well to dissolve. Reduce the heat to low, add the cinnamon and orange blossom water and heat through at a gentle simmer 3 to 4 minutes. Remove the pan from the heat and leave it to cool so the egg will not scramble when it's added.

5 Meanwhile, put the cream and the remaining sugar in a mixing bowl and whisk until the mixture forms soft peaks. Sprinkle in the coconut and gently fold to incorporate.

6 Add the egg to the cool milk mixture and whisk to combine. Ladle the mixture into the baking dish and spread the whipped cream over the top.

7 Bake in the oven 15 minutes, or until everything is bubbling and the top is golden. If necessary, place the pudding under a hot broiler the last 1 to 2 minutes to brown the top. Remove the dish from the oven and leave to stand for a couple of minutes. Serve warm.

Wild Orchid ice cream in phyllo cups

SERVES 6
PREPARATION TIME: 40 minutes,
  plus freezing
COOKING TIME: 15 minutes

3 cups whole milk

2 teaspoons salep flour or cornstarch

¼ teaspoon mastic powder
  or 2 small mastic tears (see page
  209), ground with a mortar and
  pestle, or ¼ teaspoon xanthan
  gum

¾ cup superfine sugar

1 teaspoon rosewater

2 tablespoons roughly chopped
  shelled pistachios, plus extra
  for sprinkling

3 sheets phyllo pastry dough,
  thawed if frozen

3 tablespoons butter

edible dried rose petals, to decorate
  (optional)

Salep flour, which gives this ice cream its light and elastic consistency, is milled from the dried tubers of a species of wild orchid found in the Anatolian plateau. These tubers apparently resemble the testicles of a fox, and this gave the flour its name! It's widely thought to be an aphrodisiac.

1 Pour 1½ cups of the milk into a small mixing bowl, add the salep flour and mastic powder and stir to dissolve.

2 Place a large pan over medium heat. Add the remaining milk and the sugar and whisk well to dissolve the sugar. Bring the mixture to a boil, then gradually pour the salep and milk mixture into the hot milk as you continue to whisk vigorously, gently simmering the mixture over low heat 5 minutes. Make sure the mixture does not rise up in the pan and overflow.

3 Remove the pan from the heat and mix in the rosewater and pistachios. Transfer to a freezersafe bowl and leave to cool completely, then cover and chill in the refrigerator.

4 Once the mixture is chilled, transfer it to the freezer 45 minutes, then remove and whisk well to break up all the ice crystals while incorporating as much air as possible to yield a creamier, fluffier end result. Return the mixture to the freezer 30 minutes, then remove and repeat the process again, breaking up all the ice crystals that have developed. Repeat two or three more times until completely frozen. This should take about 8 hours. You might find your whisk will no longer do the job as the ice cream hardens, in which case a spatula makes a good substitute.

5 Heat the oven to 350°F. Remove the sheets of phyllo dough from their packaging and cover them quickly with a damp dish towel.

6 Melt the butter in a small saucepan and lightly brush six cups of a muffin pan with some of it. Brush one phyllo sheet with more melted butter, add another layer on top, brush that one with butter and then repeat with the final layer. Cut the stack into six 6- x 5-inch rectangles, then gently press these rectangles into the greased muffin pan so they form cup shapes.

7 Bake the phyllo cups in the oven 6 to 8 minutes until golden brown. Lift the phyllo cups out of the pan and leave to cool. Fill each cup with a scoop of ice cream, sprinkle with pistachios and rose petals, if using, and serve.

ginger & molasses semolina marble cake

SERVES 4
PREPARATION TIME: 25 minutes
COOKING TIME: 50 minutes

½ cup (1 stick) butter

2 cups fine semolina

¼ cup superfine sugar

1 teaspoon baking soda

1⅓ cups plain yogurt

3¼-inch piece gingerroot, peeled and shredded

zest of 1 lemon

2 teaspoons date or carob molasses

⅓ cup blanched almonds

FOR THE SYRUP (OPTIONAL)

½ cup plus 2 tablespoons superfine sugar

1 teaspoon lemon juice

1 teaspoon orange blossom water

I've broken with tradition by adding molasses and ginger to this classic egg-free cake, and reducing the amount of syrup. Don't use Greek yogurt in this recipe, because it's too thick.

1 Heat the oven to 350°F. Grease an 8½-inch square baking pan with a little butter and line the bottom with parchment paper. Melt the remaining butter in a small saucepan, then set aside to cool.

2 Put the semolina, sugar and baking soda in a large mixing bowl. Pour in the melted butter and rub well with your fingers to combine.

3 Pour the yogurt into a pitcher, add the ginger and lemon zest and mix well. Pour the mixture over the semolina mixture and mix again.

4 Put the date molasses in a ramekin and dilute it with a few drops of water, so that it will be easier to drizzle off the teaspoon.

5 Spoon one-third of the semolina mixture into the prepared baking pan and shake gently to even out the surface, then drizzle one-third of the diluted molasses over the top. Repeat with another third of the semolina mixture and molasses. Top with the remaining mixture and molasses.

6 Using a skewer, knife or fork, gently swirl the mixture around in the baking pan a few times to create a marbled effect. Don't overmix. Smooth the surface, then, using a sharp knife, score the surface into diamond or square patterns (you'll have to slice again after baking, but this is to make sure the almonds will not be randomly placed), then place an almond in the middle of each diamond or square. Bake the cake in the oven 30 to 45 minutes until a skewer inserted into the middle comes out clean.

7 Meanwhile, if making the syrup, put 4 tablespoons water, the sugar, lemon juice and orange blossom water in a heavy-bottomed saucepan over medium heat and stir well. Bring to a boil and keep at a rolling ball about 5 minutes, stirring often until well incorporated, thickened and syrupy. Stir well and set aside.

8 Remove the cake from the oven, leave to cool for a few minutes, then turn it out onto a plate. Gently peel off the parchment paper. Slice into diamonds or squares, as marked earlier. Taste a small piece, adding syrup if liked.

baklawa

SERVES 8
PREPARATION TIME: 30 minutes,
  plus resting
COOKING TIME: 30 minutes

½ cup plus 2 tablespoons superfine
  sugar

juice of ½ lemon

2 cups blanched almonds

2 cups shelled pistachios

1 teaspoon ground cinnamon

1 teaspoon orange blossom water

½ cup (1 stick) unsalted butter

14 sheets phyllo pastry dough,
  thawed if frozen

Baklawa refer to a whole host of sweets prepared using phyllo pastry dough and which come in differing shapes.

1 Put the sugar, ½ cup water and the lemon juice in a heavy-bottomed saucepan and heat over medium heat. Stir well, then bring to a boil and keep at a rolling boil about 5 minutes, stirring often, until thick and syrupy. Stir well and set aside to cool.

2 Toast the almonds in a heavy-bottomed pan over medium heat 1 to 2 minutes until golden brown and fragrant, shaking the pan often.

3 Put the pistachios in a heatproof bowl and pour boiling water over. Leave 1 to 2 minutes to let the skins loosen. Strain and then rub them dry with a dish towel. Discard the skins, then rinse the pistachios under cold running water. Pat the pistachios dry with a clean dish towel.

4 Put the toasted almonds and pistachios in a small food processor and blitz until they are roughly chopped, then tip into a mixing bowl. Add half of the syrup and the cinnamon and mix well to combine. Add the orange blossom water to the remaining syrup.

5 Heat the oven to 350°F. Grease a 15- x 10-inch baking sheet with a little butter. Melt the rest of the butter in a small pan.

6 Remove the sheets of phyllo dough from their plastic packaging and cover them quickly with a damp dish towel to stop them drying out, uncovering each one only when it's needed.

7 Place one sheet of dough in the pan, trimming to fit, if necessary, and brush with melted butter. Repeat until you have finished a first layer of 6 sheets of phyllo. Spread the nut mixture evenly over the top. Layer the remaining phyllo dough sheets on top of the filling as before. (It's customary to have fewer sheets on the bottom layer.) Brush more butter on top of the last sheet, then pour in any remaining butter.

8 With a sharp knife, cut the pastry into elongated diamonds with 1¼-inch sides or into rectangles that are 1¼ inches on the long sides.

9 Bake in the oven 20 minutes, or until the top is light golden and crisp. Remove from the oven and pour as much of the remaining syrup as you like over the top; or if you have a very sweet tooth, you can use it all. Leave it to sit, uncovered, a couple of hours before serving. Store it in an airtight container up to 2 weeks.

ma'amoul shortbread cookies

MAKES 26
PREPARATION TIME: 45 minutes,
  plus chilling and resting
COOKING TIME: 15 minutes

1 cup semolina, plus extra
  for dusting

¼ cup farina (potato starch)

2 tablespoons sugar

¼ teaspoon ground mahlab or
  ground almonds

5 tablespoons butter, melted

1 tablespoon orange blossom water

confectioners' sugar, to dust

PISTACHIO FILLING
¼ cup shelled pistachios

1 tablespoon sugar

¼ teaspoon orange blossom water

WALNUT FILLING
⅓ cup walnut pieces

1 ½ tablespoons sugar

¼ teaspoon orange blossom water

DATE & WALNUT FILLING
¼ cup pitted dates

4 or 5 walnuts

a pinch ground nutmeg

1 teaspoon butter, melted

These cookies are traditionally created using three beautiful wooden molds, each engraved to identify their fillings.

1 Put the semolina, farina, sugar and mahlab in a mixing bowl. Add the melted butter along with the orange blossom water and beat well. Knead the mixture 3 to 4 minutes, working it into a pliable dough. Cover with plastic wrap and chill in the refrigerator 2 hours.

2 Meanwhile, prepare the fillings. For the pistachio filling, put the pistachios, sugar and orange blossom water in a small food processor or blender. Whiz 1 minute to form a rough paste. Transfer to a bowl.

3 For the walnut filling, put the walnuts, sugar and orange blossom water in the washed small food processor or blender. Whiz 1 minute to form a rough paste. Transfer to a bowl.

4 For the date and walnut filling, put the dates, walnuts and nutmeg in the washed food processor or blender. Melt the butter and add to the mixture, then whiz 1 minute to form a rough paste. Transfer to a bowl.

5 Remove the dough from the refrigerator and leave to rest at room temperature about 20 minutes before kneading 2 minutes.

6 Divide the dough into three even-size portion and roll out each piece into a long, thin, rod-like shape. Pinch small lumps of the dough (about 1-inch pieces), and flatten them with your palms, making sure each is very thin but not so thin it will tear.

7 Dust the ma'amoul mold cavities with semolina and then invert and tap gently to remove the excess. Gently flatten the dough into each mold cavity and add the relevant filling. Bring the edges together and seal well, then flatten the surface to create a level bottom for the cookie to sit on, pinching off any excess dough. Gently release by tapping the mold on the countertop. Repeat until you have made about eight pistachio cookies, eight walnut cookies and ten date and walnut cookies (which are smaller). Each of your cookies should be clearly stamped with its design.

8 Heat the oven to 400°F. Dust a cookie sheet with semolina and place the cookies on it. Bake 10 to 15 minutes for the larger cookies and 8 to 10 minutes for the smaller ones until the sides are slightly golden in color. Leave to cool, then dust with confectioners' sugar and serve.

Note: I like to add the filling using the mold because I find it yields more consistent results. Alternatively, flatten the dough in the palm of your hand while making a hole in it, then stuff it with the filling, seal the edges, roll it into a ball, then finally press it into a mold.

date fudge

SERVES 4
PREPARATION TIME: 45 minutes,
 plus setting and cooling
COOKING TIME: 20 minutes

1 cup less 1 tablespoon walnut
 halves, plus an extra ½ cup
 chopped walnuts

3 cups dried pitted dates

1 ¼ cups (2 ½ sticks) unsalted butter

2 ½ cups less 2 tablespoons
 all-purpose flour

½ cup confectioners' sugar

1 teaspoon ground cinnamon

½ teaspoon ground cardamom

a pinch fine sea salt

⅓ cup shelled pistachios

⅓ cup blanched almonds

This delicate confection tends to crumble between your fingers, so make sure you have a plate or a napkin on hand to put it on. It's so moreish you will want to chase every last crumb.

1 Toast the walnut halves in a heavy-bottomed pan over medium heat 2 to 3 minutes until golden brown and fragrant, shaking the pan often.

2 Stuff a toasted walnut into each date and then pack them tightly in an 8-inch baking pan, 1 ¼ inches deep.

3 Melt the butter in a deep heavy-bottomed saucepan over medium-low heat, then add the flour, confectioners' sugar, cinnamon, cardamom and salt and stir constantly 10 to 15 minutes, until the mixture resembles a smooth golden caramel.

4 Pour the mixture over the dates and smooth out with the back of a metal spoon. Leave to set 20 minutes.

5 Grind the walnut pieces, pistachios and almonds separately using a mortar and pestle. Sprinkle a thin layer of pistachios over the top of the fudge, then one of walnuts and finally almonds, then repeat until all the nuts have been used. Press the nuts down with your hands so they stick to the fudge. Leave to cool completely, then, using a sharp knife, cut into small squares or diamonds to serve.

date & tahini truffles

SERVES 4
PREPARATION TIME: 20 minutes
COOKING TIME: 1 minute

12 pitted dates

2 tablespoons tahini

⅛ teaspoon ground cardamom

2 teaspoons shelled macadamias

2 teaspoons sesame seeds

2 teaspoons shredded coconut

½ teaspoon ground coffee

Known as both an aphrodisiac and the poor man's food, there are more than 400 varieties of dates available in Iraq. These include soft and semisoft, or dry dates, also known as bread dates. The tahini is a wonderful nutty addition to this recipe. The truffles are suitable for gluten- and dairy-free eaters. Listed below are just some ideas for coatings, which you can, of course, adapt to your taste.

1 Put the dates, tahini and cardamom in a food processor and whiz 1 to 2 minutes to create an oily paste. Put the mixture in the refrigerator 10 minutes to help it firm up.

2 Meanwhile, blend the macadamias to a powder, using either a mini blender or a mortar and pestle.

3 Toast the sesame seeds in a heavy-bottomed pan over medium heat 1 minute, or until golden and fragrant, shaking the pan often.

4 Mold the date paste into 12 equal, round balls, each about ¾ inch in diameter. Put four small, shallow bowls on the countertop and put a different coating in each one: toasted sesame seeds, shredded coconut, ground macadamia and ground coffee. Roll three truffle balls in each of the flavorings until they are well coated. You might find you need to apply gentle pressure to get the coconut to stick. Transfer to a plate and serve.

Note: If you're not planning on eating the truffles shortly after making them, transfer to a rigid plastic container lined with parchment paper and store in the refrigerator up to 1 week.

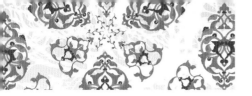

turkish delight

SERVES 4
PREPARATION TIME: 40 minutes
COOKING TIME: 1 ½ hours

2-inch piece gingerroot, peeled and grated

4 cups plus 2 tablespoons superfine sugar

juice of 1 lemon

1⅔ cups cornstarch

1 teaspoon cream of tartar

½ cup finely chopped ready-to-eat dried apricots

1 tablespoon lime juice

2 tablespoons shredded coconut

1 teaspoon rosewater

3 tablespoons shelled pistachios, roughly chopped

dried edible rose petals (optional)

⅔ cup confectioners' sugar

This recipe is more zesty and a lot less sickly than the Turkish delight you might be used to, with a texture that is very jellylike and melt-in-the-mouth. Have all your flavorings prepared and easily accessible before you start cooking. You don't want to be rushing around looking for these while your Turkish delight mixture solidifies in the saucepan…

1 You will need up to three heavy-bottomed saucepans and up to three 8-inch square silicone or rigid plastic containers, depending on the number of flavors you want to make. Line the containers with parchment paper and have the saucepans to hand.

2 Put the grated ginger in a ramekin, add 2 tablespoons boiling water and set aside to steep.

3 Meanwhile, to make the sugar syrup, put the sugar, 1 ½ cups water and the lemon juice in a heavy-bottomed saucepan. Put a candy thermometer in the liquid and bring it to a boil, stirring often, until the temperature reaches 230°F (soft-ball stage). Remove the pan from the heat and set aside to cool.

4 Put ½ cup of the cornstarch, the cream of tartar and 3 ¼ cups water into another heavy-bottomed saucepan and stir it very gently over low heat. The mixture will initially develop into a gooey ball. Be gentle when you stir it, because it has resistant characteristics; with patience the mixture will dissolve and become milky without any lumps.

5 Now, increase the heat to medium and stir the mixture constantly, concentrating fully on the job at hand, as you bring it to a gentle simmer and it reaches a creamy consistency without any lumps. Don't let it boil or it will turn into a thick, rubbery paste. (If this happens, you will need to make the cornstarch mixture again.)

6 As soon as you feel it starting to stick to the bottom of the pan, remove the pan from the heat. Quickly pour it into the sugar syrup, stirring as you do so until the mixtures are well combined. At first the mixture will be milky white, but as you continue to stir, it should become clear. Bring the mixture to a boil, stirring gently to remove any lumps, and making sure the mixture is well combined and does not collect and harden around the edge of the pan.

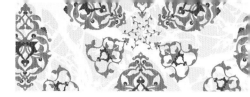

7 After a while, the mixture should start becoming clearer and then eventually (after 40 minutes or so of stirring) it will develop a yellowish hue and a thicker texture. To test for readiness, scoop out a little with a spoon and leave it to cool on a cold plate: after a few minutes, it should wrinkle when you run a finger over it.

8 If you are making only one flavor, remove the pan from the heat, and stir in the chosen ingredients to combine (see below), then pour the flavored mixture into a lined container. If you are using several flavor combinations, you will need to divide the mixture between the required number of saucepans.

9 Place the pans over medium heat and, once they are heated through, divide the mixture evenly among them and mix in the flavorings accordingly (see below). The reason for heating the pan or pans is because the cold would "shock" the mixture, quickly hardening it and making mixing anything into it difficult.

10 For ginger and apricot: drizzle 1 tablespoon of the ginger liquid (or more to taste) and sprinkle the chopped apricot over. Stir to combine, then spread out to form a flat layer in one of the lined containers.

11 For lime and coconut: drizzle the lime juice and sprinkle the shredded coconut over. Stir to combine, then spread out to form a flat layer in the second lined container.

12 For rose and pistachio: drizzle the rosewater and sprinkle the chopped pistachios and rose petals, if using, over. Stir to combine, then spread out to form a flat layer in the third container.

13 Leave all the Tukish delight to cool at room temperature, uncovered, overnight. The following day, sift the confectioners' sugar with the remaining cornstarch to create a dusting mixture. Generously dust a countertop and then tip out one portion of the Turkish delight onto it. Sprinkle enough dusting mixture over until the Turkish delight is no longer sticky to handle. Powder the edge of a very sharp knife with some of the dusting mixture and cut the Turkish delight into cubes. Repeat with the other flavors.

14 Put the Turkish delight cubes into paper bags, separated into flavors. Sprinkle in a little of the dusting mixture, then toss the Turkish delight pieces so all the exposed sides are covered.

Note: Don't store the Turkish delight in an airtight container, because it will release moisture, making the sweets sticky.

mint & gunpowder tea

SERVES 4
PREPARATION TIME: 5 minutes

**1 teabag gunpowder tea
or green tea**

8 mint sprigs

about 3 tablespoons sugar, to taste

Mint tea is so popular in Morocco it's served after every meal and has been coined "Berber whisky," because it's served at every social gathering. There is an art form that comes with pouring the tea: the higher the pour the better, so a light foam develops on the surface.

1 Pour 4 cups boiling water into a large teapot, add the teabag and the mint sprigs and leave the tea to brew 2 to 3 minutes.

2 Pour the tea into individual Moroccan tea glasses or mugs and serve with sugar to taste.

café blanc

SERVES 4
PREPARATION TIME: 2 minutes

4 teaspoons orange blossom water

1 tablespoon honey (optional)

This is not coffee as you know it, but rather a soothing and digestive herbal tea, popular in Lebanon and Syria, made from hot water subtly scented with orange blossom essence and sweetened with honey. Try it just before bedtime. I prefer it unsweetened.

1 Pour 4 cups boiling water into a large teapot, add the orange blossom water and honey, if using, and mix well to combine.

2 Pour the liquid into individual glasses or mugs and serve.

middle eastern & north african pantry

Aleppo pepper closely resembling the Ancho in flavor, hails from Aleppo, Syria. They are a bright red, mildly spicy pepper, with a high oil content and a hint of fruity sweetness with earthy, smoky tones. Aleppo pepper paste is difficult to find in the West though varying qualities of crushed flakes can be found in most Middle Eastern stores and sourced online.

Allspice (the dried unripe berries of the *Pimenta dioica* plant), is indispensable in Lebanese cuisine. It's used to flavor a variety of stews and dishes and is frequently the only spice used.

Arak is Lebanon's national drink —a clear, colorless, unsweetened, aniseed-flavored alcohol distilled from grapes.

Argan oil is a nutty-tasting oil that comes from the fruit of the argan tree. It has been used by the Berber people for centuries for its medicinal properties and to enhance their dishes. It's used in Morocco in tagines and couscous. It's also mixed with honey and eaten with bread or pancakes.

Barberries are beautiful, red, jewellike dried fruits that are bursting with tartness. If you cannot find them, dried cranberries are a suitable substitute.

Black limes/dried limes (*limu amani*) are dried in the sun until they become very hard and turn black. They lend a unique sharp, astringent flavor to fishy stews, soups and dishes rich in legumes and meats. They might be punctured, broken open or ground to a powder before being used in a recipe.

Bulgur wheat, also known as *burghul*, is a cereal food made from different wheat species, usually durum wheat. It's sold parboiled, dried and with the bran partially removed. It's available in four grinds or sizes: fine (1), medium (2), coarse (3) and extra-coarse (4). The bulgur you see labeled in most stores as "fine" is, in fact, close to "medium." So if the grade is important, it's best to source your bulgur from a Middle Eastern/ethnic store, which usually carry several grades. Bulgur is considered more nutritious than white rice and couscous because of its high fiber and vitamin and mineral content. It's one of the ingredients used in tabbouleh (though only sparingly). The coarser varieties are preferred in stuffings and pilafs.

Couscous can be bought in instant and precooked versions, but ignore them as these will turn into mush when cooked. Instead, choose noninstant couscous (available at most Middle Eastern grocery stores). It takes longer to cook and is traditionally steamed in a couscoussière, which houses the necessary mesh-steamer inside a pot in which a flavorful broth or stew is simmered. If you cannot find a couscoussière, use a regular steamer and line the steamer basket or colander with cheesecloth or a dish towel. Couscous is traditionally served alongside a tagine or stew.

Dried edible rose petals have a delicate sweet fragrance and usually come in pink, lilac or red. They are best kept in an airtight container, because they lose their aroma quickly.

Freekeh is an ancient grain and cereal food made from green wheat native to many parts of the Middle East and North Africa. It has a nutty undertone and a smoky aroma. It's high in fiber, protein, vitamins and minerals. It can be purchased cracked and whole, and might require careful cleaning to rid it of any stones. Freekeh has wonderful smoky, earthy tones, and so some brands are preferable for certain dishes that require more subtle flavors.

Gram flour can be made from split peas (*channa dal*) or chickpeas. Here I use the chickpea variety. Most gram flours are from chickpeas, but it's always worth checking.

Kishk is a fine, powdery cereal that is a mixture of bulgur wheat that has been fermented, usually with yogurt. To many people it's a treasured acquired taste, with its musky, cheeselike, sour tones. It can be found at only some Middle Eastern grocery stores.

Mahlab is a spice derived from the sour cherry pits of the St. Lucia tree (*Prunus mahaleb*). The kernels from these cherries are ground to an aromatic powder. The flavor is a combination of bitter almond and cherry. Mahlab is used for its unique taste, ground or whole, to flavor different dishes around the Middle East. If the recipe calls for actual sour cherries (such as the Venison & Sour Cherry Nests on page 30), use morello cherries.

Mastic is a gum and an aromatic resin that is cultivated from the bark of the Mediterranean mastic tree. It's crushed and used in powder form in many desserts in parts of the Mediterranean and across the Middle East. Use mastic tears (drop-shaped pieces of the resin) or powder sparingly, because the flavor the gum imparts can become overpowering.   .

Moghrabieh, a form of rolled semolina, like couscous, but much larger, cooks unevenly because the grains are rolled into different size balls. These starchy balls swell and become soft and chewy when cooked and are fantastic at absorbing the flavors of the dish they are cooked in. If you're unable to find moghrabieh, then fregola can
be substituted. I like to steam the moghrabieh when I cook it, which helps to keep the grains distinct.

Orange blossom water is a clear, fragrant water distilled from

macerated blossom flowers of the Seville orange. It's believed that a spoon of orange blossom water diluted with water and some sugar or honey, otherwise known as Café Blanc (see page 207), can increase your heart rate. It's a traditional ingredient in Middle Eastern desserts.

Pomegranate molasses is a syrup made by boiling down the juice of pomegranates until it reduces to a thick, crimson-brown liquid. It's used in meats, stews, salads and as a condiment. The flavor is both sweet and tart.

Rosewater is a clear, fragrant water distilled from macerated fresh wild roses. It's a traditional ingredient in Middle Eastern desserts and is used alone or in combination with orange blossom water in many desserts.

Salep flour is milled from the dried tubers of a wild orchid species found in the Anatolian plateau. It's prominently used in both a popular milk and spice beverage of the same name and also a light ice cream. Salep can be quite difficult to find and expensive, but you can replace it with cornstarch or even ground mastic gum.

Smen (or *samneh*, *semneh*) is an oil made from clarified butter that is aged and sometimes buried underground. It has a very distinctive rancid aroma and pungent flavor. As the aroma becomes stronger with age, the more prized the smen becomes as a reflection of a family's wealth. Still considered a delicacy in Morocco, it's an intricate part of traditional tagines and other dishes.

Sumac is a tangy, deep red or burgundy spice derived from the dried berries of the sumac bush. It's used along with lemon or in place of lemon to add a tart flavor to dishes such as Spinach & Sumac Turnovers (see page 37), as well as meats, fried eggs and dips. It can also be added to other spices, like the Wild Thyme Mixture (see page 220).

Tahini, a paste of ground sesame seeds, is one of the main ingredients used in hummus b tahini and other Middle Eastern dishes. It can be made into a sauce called Tarator (see page 220) by thinning it down with water and flavoring it with lemon juice, salt and garlic. It's a popular condiment in many Middle Eastern dishes.

Tamarind is a souring agent that lends a very distinctive flavor to curries and stews. It's sold in several forms and can be found in large supermarkets, as well as in Asian, Spanish and Middle Eastern grocery stores. I prefer to use block rather than concentrate tamarind, since it's nearly identical to fresh pods, but easier to use because you don't have to break it out of its shell. It's also more tart and flavorsome.

Verjuice, the unfermented sour juice extracted from semiripe grapes, adds a wonderfully delicate, sweet-tangy tone to dishes, salads and reductions. It's available in some supermarkets and Middle Eastern delicatessens.

Wheat berries (whole unprocessed wheat kernels), are high in fiber with a chewy texture, and although they take time to cook, they don't need to be soaked.

basic recipes & methods

BASIC RECIPES

CHERMOULA

I've had an unremitting crush on chermoula for decades. While the name points to the North African condiment, my father has been making a version of this scrumptious sauce to stuff his infamous Silantro-Stuffed Trout for years. If you like cilantro and love garlic, then you'll quickly find chermoula creeping into plenty of your dishes. It's very versatile, lending itself equally well to tagines (see page 144) and marinades.

Serves 4
Preparation time: 10 minutes
Cooking time: 2 minutes

¼ teaspoon cumin seeds
2 handfuls cilantro leaves (or a combination of cilantro and parsley leaves)
2 tablespoons dill leaves
2-inch piece gingerroot, peeled and roughly chopped
2 chilies, seeded and roughly chopped
2 wedges Preserved Lemon (see page 212), flesh removed and the peel roughly chopped
8 garlic cloves, crushed with the blade of a knife
4 tablespoons olive oil, plus extra for storing
sea salt

1 Toast the cumin seeds in a heavy-bottomed frying pan over medium heat 1 to 2 minutes until fragrant, shaking the pan often.

2 Put all the ingredients, except for the oil, into a food processor and pulse to combine into a rough paste. Pour in the oil and pulse once more to combine. Season to taste with salt. Use as required.

3 Transfer any unused chermoula to an airtight container and pour a thin layer of olive oil over the top. Seal and store in the refrigerator up to 10 days.

HARISSA

Another North African condiment, this fiery sauce can be served separately, but also makes its way into many North African dishes. This recipe is merely a guideline, and I recommend you adjust the ingredients to give the flavor that best suits your taste, then use it in proportion to your personal heat scale, depending on the recipe. Harissa will keep, covered, in the refrigerator up to 3 weeks.

Serves 4
Preparation time: 15 minutes, plus soaking and macerating
Cooking time: 2 minutes

15 whole hot, dried chilies
4 tablespoons olive oil, plus extra for storing
¼ teaspoon coriander seeds
¼ teaspoon caraway seeds
¼ teaspoons cumin seeds
8 garlic cloves, crushed
1 tablespoon tomato paste

1 Put the dried chilies in a small heatproof bowl, cover with boiling water and leave to soak about 20 minutes. Drain the chilies and pat dry on paper towels. Slice off the stems, then remove the seeds, if you like, and finely chop. Transfer to a small bowl, pour the oil over and leave to macerate 1 hour.

2 Toast the coriander, caraway and cumin seeds in a heavy-bottomed pan over medium heat 1 to 2 minutes until fragrant, shaking the pan often.

3 Put all the ingredients, except the tomato paste, in a mini blender and puree to a fine paste, stopping occasionally to scrape down the side. Stir in the tomato paste, then transfer to a small, sterilized glass jar. Cover with a thin layer of oil and seal.

4 Keep in the refrigerator, topping up with more oil after each use.

ADVIEH

There are two variations of this spice mix.

ADVIEH 1

Makes: 1 tablespoon
Preparation time: 2 minutes
Cooking time: 2 minutes

seeds from 4 cardamom pods
1 teaspoon cumin seeds
1 teaspoon turmeric seeds
½ teaspoon caraway seeds
1 teaspoon ground cinnamon

1 Toast the cardamom, cumin and turmeric seeds in a heavy-bottomed pan over medium heat 1 to 2 minutes until fragrant, shaking the pan often.

2 Grind the spices and caraway seeds using a mortar and pestle. Combine with the cinnamon. Store in an airtight container in a cool, dark place up to 3 months.

ADVIEH 2

Makes: about 4 tablespoons
Preparation time: 2 minutes

1 tablespoon ground pistachios
½ teaspoon ground dried edible rose petals (see page 208)
½ teaspoon saffron threads
1 teaspoon ground cardamom
1 teaspoon ground cinnamon

1 Mix together all of the ingredients until combined. Use as directed or store in an airtight container in a cool, dark place up to 3 months.

LEBANESE SEVEN SPICES

This is a popular spice mixture in Lebanon. It works wonderfully as a rub on lamb and beef.

Makes: 2 tablespoons
Preparation time: 2 minutes

1 teaspoon ground cloves
1 teaspoon ground allspice
1 teaspoon ground fenugreek
1 teaspoon grated nutmeg
1 teaspoon ground ginger
1 teaspoon ground cinnamon
1 teaspoon freshly ground black pepper

1 Mix all the ingredients together and use as directed. Store in a cool, dark place up to 3 months.

HERB BUTTER

A flavor-packed finishing touch for main dishes.

Serves 4
Preparation time: 5 minutes
Cooking time: 10 minutes

7 tablespoons butter
5 garlic cloves, finely chopped
1 handful cilantro leaves, finely chopped
1 handful mint leaves, finely chopped
sea salt and freshly ground black pepper

1 Melt the butter in a heavy-bottomed skillet over medium heat until it sizzles. Add the garlic and cook 1 minute, or until aromatic.

2 Add the herbs, mix well and cook about 5 minutes until fragrant. Season to taste with salt and pepper.

VEGETABLE STOCK

Homemade stock is easy to make and a great way to use up vegetables that are past their best. Sweating rather than browning the veg gives the best result, I find.

Makes: about 6½ cups
Preparation time: 15 minutes
Cooking time: 45 minutes

1 tablespoon olive oil
5 white mushrooms, wiped clean and roughly chopped
4 garlic cloves, crushed with the blade of a knife
3 celery sticks, roughly chopped with leaves reserved
2 carrots, roughly chopped
1 fennel bulb, roughly chopped
1 leek, roughly chopped
1 onion, roughly chopped
1 bay leaf
1 handful parsley leaves
1 thyme sprig (optional)
1 rosemary sprig (optional)
a pinch ground allspice
a pinch sea salt

1 Put the oil in a large stockpot over medium heat. Add all the ingredients, then cover and sweat 2 to 3 minutes. Pour in 2 quarts water. Cover and bring to a boil, then reduce the heat to low and simmer 35 minutes. Strain, discarding the solids. Use as called for in a recipe, or cool and freeze any remaining stock.

PRESERVED LEMONS

I suggest you prepare these as soon as possible, because they are very important to the Moroccan kitchen and are called for in several recipes. Once you've tried cooking with them, you'll want to include them in your cooking forever. Follow the 3-week recipe for the best results, but if time is short, opt for the 5-day version instead, and if time is really short, use good-quality bought preserved lemons. You might occasionally notice a white substance forming on the top of the lemons. Although this is harmless, rinse it off before using.

PRESERVED LEMONS IN 3 WEEKS

Serves 4
Preparation time: 10 minutes, plus 3 weeks preserving

3 pounds lemons (about 16)
8 tablespoons sea salt

1 Wash 8 of the lemons well and pat dry thoroughly. Soften them by rolling them back and forth on the countertop. (I recommend doing this whenever you use a lemon, because it encourages the juices to run freely.) Using a sharp knife, slice off any protruding stems and then slice the lemons vertically, almost into quarters, stopping before you reach the bottom. The lemon quarters will still be attached at the bottom by about 1 inch of peel.

2 Gently ease the lemon quarters apart without tearing them at the bottom, then stuff the middle of each lemon generously with 1 tablespoon of the sea salt.

3 Pack the lemons tightly into a sterilized 1-quart preserving jar, squashing them down so that any juices are released.

4 Juice the remaining 8 lemons, then pour the juice over the lemon wedges to cover, adding more lemon juice, if necessary, to keep them submerged. Leave about ½-inch air space.

5 Seal the jar tightly and store at room temperature. Each day for the first 3 days, turn the jar upside down occasionally. After that, leave 3 weeks before using, so the lemon peels have had time to soften. Once opened, they can be stored in the refrigerator 6 to 12 months.

6 To use, remove a lemon or just detach a wedge, depending on the recipe, and rinse thoroughly in water to remove the excess salt. Most of the recipes in this book will call for the peel only, but the pulp is fine to use for its taste, if you like.

PRESERVED LEMONS IN 5 DAYS

Serves 4
Preparation time: 10 minutes, plus 5 days preserving
Cooking time: 30 minutes

1 ½ pounds lemons (about 8)
6 tablespoons sea salt

1 Prepare all the lemons following steps 1 and 2 of the 3-week version.

2 Put 4 cups water in a large, stainless steel saucepan over medium heat. Add the lemons (and a small heatproof plate, if needed, to keep them submerged). Bring to a boil, then simmer about 30 minutes until soft. Remove the pan from the heat and leave the lemons to cool.

3 Once cool, transfer the lemons to a sterilized 1-quart preserving jar and pour some of the cooking juices over to cover.

4 Seal the jar tightly and store at room temperature 5 days. Each day, turn the jar upside down occasionally. Once opened, they can be stored in the refrigerator 6 to 12 months. Use as for the 3-week version.

SAFFRON LIQUID

Saffron is an essential ingredient in the Persian kitchen. Although it is a delicately aromatic and mildly pungent spice, using too much will yield an overpowering medicinal taste, so use it sparingly. The deeper the color of the threads, the better the quality. Ground saffron can easily be adulterated, so I recommend using saffron threads. Store the saffron threads in an airtight jar in a cool, dark place. Increase the quantities based on requirement, and store any extra saffron liquid in an airtight container, in the refrigerator, for up to a week.

Makes 1 tablespoon
Preparation time: 5 minutes, plus infusing
Cooking time: 30 seconds

10 saffron threads

1 Toast the saffron threads in a heavy-bottomed pan over medium heat 30 seconds, or until fragrant, shaking the pan often.

2 Transfer the saffron to a mortar and leave to cool 1 to 2 minutes before grinding them into a powder.

3 Mix the ground saffron with 1 tablespoon boiling water and set aside to infuse at least 1 hour until a rich orange hue appears before using. The color and flavor will continue to develop for about 12 hours.

PANEER CHEESE

Paneer is a fresh cheese with a creamy taste and texture that is set with acid rather than rennet, making it completely vegetarian. It's somewhat similar to ricotta cheese, and salt is not traditionally added. Because it's a nonmelting cheese, it can be fried. Note, however, you do need to allow two days for the yogurt to sour.

Makes about 1 cup
Preparation time: 15 minutes, plus up to 2 days souring, 1 hour resting and up to 2½ hours straining
Cooking time: 10 to 15 minutes

1½ cups plus 2 tablespoons plain yogurt
8¾ cups whole milk
½ teaspoon sea salt

1 Put the yogurt in a bowl and cover with a dish towel. Leave at room temperature 24 to 48 hours until a sample tastes sour.

2 Once the yogurt is sour, pour the milk into a heavy-bottomed saucepan and bring to a gentle boil, watching it carefully to make sure the milk does not boil over or catch on the bottom of the pan, in which case it will have to be discarded.

3 Whisk the sour yogurt well and pour it into the milk, then stir at least 5 to 10 minutes until the milk solids curdle and separate from the whey. Remove the pan from the heat and leave to rest up to 1 hour, during which time the milk will continue to curdle.

4 Meanwhile, line a colander with cheesecloth and secure it over a large bowl. Pour in the curdled milk, collecting the curd in the mesh and the whey in the bowl. If you like, you can also reserve the whey, which can be used to make ricotta, dilute yogurt drinks (see page 221), cook rice and make breads or pancakes, and can also be added to soups.

5 Gather the edges of the cheesecloth and tie it in a tight bundle. For a soft paneer, leave the bundle to hang from the sink faucet about 30 minutes. For a firmer paneer, rest the bundle in a colander that has been secured over a bowl, adding weight to it, such as a pot containing a bag of beans, and leave to strain 2 hours longer. Transfer to a bowl, cover and store in the refrigerator up to one week. Serve with a mixed herb salad.

Note: For a much quicker preparation time, you can simply squeeze the juice of 1 lemon into the milk and stir often up to 5 minutes until the milk curdles. This method, however, does not yield as much curdling or creaminess as the yogurt method.

SAVORY PASTRY DOUGH

This is the basic dough recipe for the savory pastries that grace an authentic Lebanese dinner party, buffet or meze. Use it in recipes such as the Spinach & Sumac Turnovers (see page 37) and the Ground Lamb & Onion Crescents (see page 24).

Serves 4
Preparation time: 20 minutes, plus resting
Cooking time: 1 minute

1 cup all-purpose flour, plus extra for dusting
½ teaspoon sea salt flakes
1 teaspoon sugar
4 tablespoons olive oil, plus extra for greasing
6 tablespoons milk
½ teaspoon active dry yeast

1 Sift the flour, salt and sugar into a mound on a clean countertop and create a well in the middle. Add the oil to the middle of the well and, using your hands, begin to combine with the flour until all is incorporated.

2 Heat the milk until lukewarm, then pour it into a small bowl. Sprinkle the yeast into the milk and mix thoroughly. Add the milk and yeast to the flour and oil mixture and knead about 5 minutes, dusting the countertop with flour, as necessary, until the dough is smooth and elastic and forms a ball.

3 Place the dough in a large bowl greased with a little oil and score the top with a knife to loosen the surface tension. Cover with a damp, clean dish towel and place in a warm, draft-free place about 1 hour before using.

CHELOW RICE

Some of the recipes in this book follow a two-stage Persian technique of cooking rice, in which the rice is first parboiled and then steamed. The resulting chelow (plain) rice can be eaten as it is or it can have additional ingredients added, which are layered up with the rice in the pan before the rice is steamed. These dishes are known as polow, or mixed rice.

The key to preparing this light-and-fluffy rice is to wash the loose starch out so each grain of rice remains distinct after its cooked. Next, soak the rice 30 minutes before parboiling it. Buy the best basmati rice you can afford. Although the amount of salt used might seem surprisingly large, it will be rinsed off, so the rice will not taste salty.

PARBOILED RICE (STAGE 1)

Serves 4
Preparation time: 5 minutes, plus soaking the rice
Cooking time: 5 minutes

2 cups basmati rice
3 tablespoons sea salt

1 Pick over the rice to remove any dirt or discolored grains. Wash the rice thoroughly in five or six changes of water, until it runs clear, which signals all the loose starch has been removed.

2 Pour 4 cups warm water into a large bowl and add 1 tablespoon of the salt. Add the rice and leave to soak no more than 30 minutes, running your fingers through it every so often to help loosen the grains. Drain the rice and rinse under warm water.

3 Pour 5½ cups water into a large saucepan and add the remaining salt. Bring to a boil and stir in the well-strained rice, then bring back to a boil and cook, uncovered, 3 minutes over high heat until the grains are soft on the outside but still firm in the middle. Do not stir the rice again, because this can break the grains.

4 Drain the parboiled rice in a strainer and rinse with lukewarm water, tossing the rice gently to remove the excess moisture and to separate the grains. At this point you can set the rice aside until you are ready to cook your chosen recipe, if you like. This means you can parboil the rice the day before you want it, then continue with the recipe the following day. (Once the rice is cool, it needs to be stored in the refrigerator, where it can be kept safely up to 3 days. Return to room temperature before using.)

STEAMED RICE (STAGE 2)

The oil added at this stage forms the tahdeeg ("base of the pot") layer. If you want to make the dish healthier, use less oil than suggested, for a thinner tahdeeg.

Serves 4
Preparation time: 15 minutes
Cooking time: 45 minutes

3 to 6 tablespoons sunflower oil
1 recipe quantity Parboiled Rice (see left)
4 tablespoons unsalted butter

1 Heat the oil in a heavy-bottomed saucepan over medium heat until the oil is sizzling. Using a spoon, sprinkle 4 or 5 tablespoons of the parboiled rice across the bottom of the pan. Continue sprinkling the remaining rice, building it up into a dome shape. (Tipping it all in at once will compress the rice, and the end result will not be a light and fluffy dish.)

2 Use the handle of a wooden spoon to make three holes in the rice to the bottom of the pan. Melt the butter in a small saucepan over low heat, then pour over the rice.

3 Wrap the saucepan lid in a clean dish towel and tie it into a tight knot at the handle, then cover the saucepan with the lid as tightly as you can so any steam does not escape. (The dish towel prevents the moisture from dripping into the rice and making it soggy.)

4 Reduce the heat to low and cook the rice, covered, 20 to 40 minutes longer. If you cook for just 20 minutes, the rice will be light and fluffy and the tahdeeg will be golden, although very loose; if you cook for the full 40 minutes, the rice will remain tender and fluffy, but the tahdeeg will be firmer and darker, which is how it would be eaten in the Middle East. The choice is yours.

5 When the rice is cooked, place the saucepan in 2 inches cold water in the kitchen sink and leave 1 to 2 minutes. This helps to "shock" the rice and loosen the tahdeeg.

6 Gently spoon the rice out (making sure not to disturb the tahdeeg) and sprinkle it lightly onto a dish, shaping it into a dome. Alternatively, gently tip the pan out onto the dish, allowing the rice to spill out into a mound.

7 Remove the tahdeeg by inverting the saucepan onto a plate, using a spatula to loosen it, if necessary. Serve the tahdeeg separately on a plate or on top of the rice.

VERMICELLI RICE

Rice cooked with vermicelli is a popular side dish in the Middle East. If you buy the vermicelli from a Middle Eastern store, they will most likely come already broken up, otherwise vermicelli nests can be broken up. Egyptian rice, which is short or medium grain, is traditionally used to make this dish, but basmati can be substituted. In keeping with the Persian method of preparation, it's best to rinse the rice well to remove any starch. The quantity of water needed will depend on the quality of rice used.

Serves 4
Preparation time: 10 minutes
Cooking time: 30 minutes

1 cup short- or medium-grain rice
2 tablespoons butter
1 ounce vermicelli
sea salt and freshly ground black pepper

1 Rinse the rice under cold running water until the water runs clear. Drain well and set aside.

2 Melt the butter in a heavy-bottomed saucepan over medium heat. Break the vermicelli into pieces about ¾ inch long and cook 2 to 3 minutes until golden, stirring often.

3 Add the rice to the cooked vermicelli, tossing until it is well incorporated, then pour 2 cups and 2 tablespoons boiling water over. Increase the heat to high, then cover the pan and bring to a boil. Reduce the heat to low and cook 15 to 20 minutes until all the water is absorbed and the rice is soft. Season to taste with salt and pepper before serving with other dishes.

SOAKING & COOKING CHICKPEAS

The ideal method for cooking chickpeas is to use a pressure cooker. Alternatively, follow the steps below.

Serves 4
Preparation time: 15 minutes, plus overnight soaking
Cooking time: 30 minutes to 1½ hours

1 Put the dried chickpeas in a large bowl (they will double in size), cover with two times their volume in cold water and leave to soak overnight.

2 Rinse the soaked chickpeas well under cold running water and transfer to a heavy-bottomed saucepan. Cover with water and then again by a half.

3 Bring to a boil, then reduce the heat to low, partially cover the pan and cook 30 minutes. Cover the pan fully and cook longer, depending on the results you want or what a recipe states: 30 minutes for al dente, 1 hour for tender or 1½ hours for mushy, skimming off any scum that forms with a slotted spoon. Keep an eye on the pan to make sure it does not overflow. Drain, then use as required, reserving the cooking liquid if necessary.

Note If you cannot use cooked chickpeas and have to resort to the canned variety, be sure to soak them in water 10 to 15 minutes and then rinse them well under running water to remove as much "can" flavor as possible.

LEBANESE CLOTTED CREAM

Ashta (to skim) is the Lebanese clotted cream and adds a delicious finish to many desserts.

Serves 4
Preparation time: 5 minutes
Cooking time: 5 minutes

1 tablespoon cornstarch
1 cup plus 2 tablespoons light or whipping cream

1 Put the cornstarch in a small bowl, add 1 tablespoon water and stir until completely smooth.

2 Pour the cream into a heavy-bottomed saucepan and heat over medium heat until warm. Whisk in the cornstarch mixture, stirring vigorously 3 to 5 minutes until it thickens to the consistency of clotted, or thick, cream, then remove the pan from the heat and leave the cream to cool.

3 Transfer the clotted cream to a bowl, cover and put in the refrigerator to chill until ready to use.

ROASTED VEGETABLES

Vegetables that have been roasted or chargrilled have an intense flavor and a crisp, yet juicy, texture. Choose the cooking method (gas stove, charcoal barbecue, gas barbecue or oven) that suits the recipe and the situation.

Serves 4
Preparation time: 10 minutes, plus resting
Cooking time: 20 minutes

eggplants and/or bell peppers, as required

1 Turn a gas burner to high and lean the eggplants and/or peppers, stem still on, directly over the burner, turning each one occasionally with tongs until all the sides are charred and the eggplants or peppers are soft. This should take about 5 minutes per side, or 15 to 20 minutes in total. Use as many burners as necessary.

2 Alternatively, heat a charcoal barbecue until the charcoal is burning white, turn on a gas barbecue or heat the oven to 400°F. Cook the eggplants or peppers (poke eggplants a few times if roasting in the oven, to avoid them bursting) until all the sides are charred and the flesh is soft. Remove from the heat and transfer to a sealable plastic bag, then seal and leave to rest 10 minutes.

3 Holding the stem of one eggplant or pepper at a time, use the bag to peel off the skin and any charred edges.

OPENING POMEGRANATES

Pomegranates can be one of the messiest fruits to open, making your walls look like a preschooler's canvas. The following method is efficient and makes capturing the seeds—its scarlet jewels—a more relaxed process.

1 Use the palm of your hand to roll the pomegranate on the countertop, which loosens the seeds, then cut off the pomegranate crown with a sharp knife. Score the fruit into segments, not cutting through all the way, but making sure to score just enough so you can easily peel the skin.

2 Fill a large bowl with water, put the pomegranate in the water and begin to peel apart the scored segments. Discard the skin. Gently pry the seeds apart. All the white pith will float to the top, where you can sift it off with a strainer, and the seeds will sink to the bottom.

ACCOMPANIMENTS

COUSCOUS

The Moroccan way of preparing couscous is to steam it in a couscoussière. If you cannot find a couscoussière, a very suitable alternative is to use a regular steamer and line the steamer basket with cheesecloth or a dish towel. Instant couscous, which is readily available, is more convenient because it involves only a matter of rehydrating it in boiled or simmering water. Unfortunately, though, instant couscous cannot be steamed because the long cooking time will render it to a mush. So, if you've gone to the trouble of cooking a stew, then you might as well steam the couscous at the same time. You can find noninstant couscous at most Middle Eastern grocery stores. You'll need to start cooking the couscous about 40 minutes before the stew should finish cooking.

Serves 4
Preparation time: 20 minutes
Cooking time: 35 minutes

3 ¼ cups Vegetable Stock (see page 211)
2 cups couscous
4 tablespoons olive oil or 4 teaspoons butter, softened
sea salt

1 Heat the vegetable stock until warm. Meanwhile, place the couscous in a mixing bowl, add the olive oil and rub it in with your hands to distribute the fat evenly. Add ½ cup of the stock and stir with a fork until the couscous absorbs the stock and plumps up. Season with salt to taste and break up any lumps with your fingers.

2 Pour the remaining stock into the bottom of a large steamer and place it over medium heat. Line the steamer basket or a colander with a damp dish towel or cheesecloth, then add the couscous. Fold the towel loosely over the couscous, making sure it is not compressed. Alternatively, if you're cooking a stew at the same time, place the steamer basket on top of the stewpot. Cover and seal any open edges by wrapping a dish towel or foil around it to minimize the escape of steam. Simmer 15 minutes.

3. Remove the couscous bundle from the steamer and toss the grains with a fork 1 minute. Leave to cool about 5 minutes. Gather the cloth into a bundle again and return to the steamer basket, cover and steam 15 minutes longer, or until the grains are soft. Serve with a stew, if using.

ARABIC BREAD

Arabic bread is a pivotal part of the Middle Eastern eating experience, where it is used interchangeably with utensils to create delicate bites, wraps or sandwiches and to help mop up prized stew juices. It's in quite a separate league to the thick, heavy pita breads sold in the West. Making Arabic bread at home is rewarding, and watching the air pockets develop is exciting. Sure, it's not the exact texture of commercial-grade Arabic bread, but that's precisely the point. Baking this beautiful bread is, in fact, not as difficult as you might imagine: just be sure to have a well-heated oven ready before popping the dough in.

Arabic bread has many uses. As well as being served alongside stews and other dishes with sauces, it can also be used in different ways. For example, you can also spread Wild Thyme Mixture (see page 220) and olive oil over the dough before popping it into the oven for a pizza-style snack. (See also Spiced Lamb Flatbread Pizzas, page 107.) Triangles of Arabic bread can be toasted and then used to dip into hummus, or added to Fattoush Salad (see page 61). Alternatively, the toasted bread can be crushed into large bread crumbs and then used in a dish such as Eggplant, Veal & Yogurt Crumble (see page 119).

Serves 4
Preparation time: 25 minutes, plus rising
Cooking time: 3 minutes

2½ cups white bread flour, plus extra for dusting
½ teaspoon sea salt
1 teaspoon sugar
4 tablespoons olive oil
2 teaspoons active dry yeast

1 Sift the flour into a mixing bowl, add the salt and sugar and pour in the oil, then mix well with your hands.

2 Add the yeast to ⅔ cup lukewarm water and stir until it dissolves. Pour the water and yeast mixture into the flour and oil mixture, little by little, combining it with your hands as you go, until a ball forms. Depending on the age and brand of flour, you might find that you need more or less water.

3 Transfer the dough to a well-floured countertop and continue kneading it until it is smooth and elastic. Return the dough ball to the mixing bowl, then score the top with a knife to loosen the surface tension. Cover with a damp, clean dish towel and place it in a warm, draft-free place about 1 hour until it doubles in size.

4 Once the dough has doubled in size, turn it out onto a lightly floured countertop and punch it down, then knead gently before rolling it into a log. Divide the log into four equal-size balls, each weighing about 4 ounces. Lightly flour the countertop once more and use a rolling pin to roll out each ball of dough, reflouring the countertop as necessary. For small loaves, roll out each ball of dough into a circle about 8 inches in diameter. For large loaves, roll out each ball of dough into a circle about 12 inches in diameter. Cover the loaves with a dish towel and leave to rest 10 minutes longer.

5 Meanwhile, heat the oven to 450°F and place a cookie sheet in the oven to get hot. Baking one loaf at a time, spray lightly with water and then bake 2 minutes, or until the top and edges are lightly golden and a pocket of air has formed (the cooking time depends on the heat of the oven and the thickness of the bread). Do not cook them for longer than 1 minute after the air pocket forms, or they will turn out more brittle than pliable. Leaving the breads to cool uncovered will also make them brittle, so if you are not serving them immediately, cover with a damp dish towel and store in a sealed plastic bag.

6 The breads can be kept, wrapped, in a refrigerator up to 2 or 3 days, or in a freezer up to 1 to 2 months. Allow 20–30 minutes thawing time. Alternatively, microwave briefly or bake in a hot oven a couple of minutes.

THIN FLATBREAD

Nan-e taftoon as this bread is known in Iran, is traditionally baked in hot, deep ovens called tannours. It's also a great accompaniment to many of the dishes in this book. You can enjoy a simple but very satisfying meal by pairing freshly baked flatbreads with a good white cheese and Undressed Herb Salad (see page 67). You need at least two cookie sheets to cope with how fast the breads bake.

Makes 6
Preparation time: 30 minutes, plus rising and resting
Cooking time: 25 minutes

1 teaspoon active dry yeast
3 cups white bread flour, plus extra for dusting
1 teaspoon sea salt

1 Dissolve the yeast in ¼ cup warm water in a bowl and set aside 5 minutes.

2 Meanwhile, mix the flour and salt on a clean countertop, then create a well in the middle. Add 1¾ cups warm water to the yeast water, then pour it into the well. Gradually work the liquid into the flour, mixing and kneading with your hands, until it forms a soft dough.

3 Knead the dough 10 to 15 minutes until it is very smooth and elastic and comes away from the countertop. Transfer to a lightly oiled bowl, cover with a slightly damp dish towel and leave in a warm, draft-free place 2 hours, or until it doubles in size.

4 When the dough has doubled, remove it from the bowl, place on a lightly floured countertop and punch down, kneading until it is soft and elastic. Roll the dough into a log, then divide it into six equal balls and space these out on the countertop. Score the top of each ball with a knife to loosen the surface tension. Cover with a damp, clean dish towel and leave to rest 20 minutes.

5 Once the dough is rested, heat the oven to 475°F and place a large cookie sheet in the oven to get hot. Working with one piece of dough at a time, punch it down on the floured countertop, then roll it out as thinly as possible into a 13- x 9- x ¼-inch rectangular shape to fit the cookie sheet.

6 Remove the cookie sheet from the oven and scatter some flour over it, then quickly but carefully transfer one of the thin sheets of dough to the baking sheet, stretching it just a little more, if needed, to fit the cookie sheet (but being careful not to tear it and not to burn your hand on the cookie sheet). Gently prick the surface with a fork to minimize large air pockets developing.

7 Bake 2 to 4 minutes until the dough is blistered and is a very light, golden color. The aim is for the bread to be soft with golden hints. While the first bread is baking, prepare the next one.

8 Remove the bread from the oven and place on a wire rack to cool. The bread might be slightly crisp when it first comes out of the oven, but it will soften and become pliable as it cools. Serve warm or cold.

9 Once each loaf is cold, wrap it in a damp paper towels and refrigerate; alternatively, place in a sealable plastic bag and freeze 1 to 2 months. When required, sprinkle the chilled or frozen breads with water. Microwave chilled breads 30 seconds and frozen breads 2 minutes respectively. Alternatively, you can heat the chilled bread in a nonstick skillet over medium heat 45 seconds on each side.

POTATO MATCHSTICKS

Crisp, golden matchstick-size French fries are the perfect accompaniment for many of the dishes in this book. For consistently thin results, use a mandolin on the finest julienne setting. Alternatively, use a thin sharp knife. I like to cut the fries thin and long. You can keep them in ice-cold water if you are making ahead, rather than just rinsing them, and then pat dry before frying.

Serves 4
Preparation time: 20 minutes
Cooking time: 10 minutes

1 pound 2 ounces Idaho potatoes, peeled
sunflower oil, for deep-frying
½ teaspoon sea salt

1 Slice the potatoes into thin matchsticks and rinse under cold running water to rid them of excess starch. Dry thoroughly on a clean dish towel or using a salad spinner.

2 Heat a large, deep skillet over high heat and pour in enough oil for deep-frying. Bring the temperature of the oil to 400°F. To test if the oil is hot enough, add a potato matchstick to the oil: if it floats, the oil is ready.

3 Cook in batches, if necessary, 4 to 5 minutes until crisp and light golden. Remove the matchsticks from the oil and transfer to a plate lined with paper towels to drain. Season with salt before serving.

BURNED TOMATO & CHILI JAM

Here's my take on this sweet-and savory specialty from the city of Marrakesh, which makes a very versatile accompaniment to plenty of dishes, including Shipwrecked Potato Boats (see page 41) and Artichokes with Couscous (see page 33), along with cheese and an array of tagines, flatbreads, fries and so on. I make this in big batches because it's great to have extra on hand; I've witnessed, in bewilderment, a friend shovel it down by the spoonful.

Makes about 2 cups
Preparation time: 20 minutes
Cooking time: 1 hour

2 pounds 4 ounces tomatoes, quartered
½ teaspoon coriander seeds
¼ teaspoon ground cinnamon
1 small red onion, sliced into ¼-inch rings
2 red chilies, seeded (optional) and thinly sliced
5 fat garlic cloves, crushed with the blade of a knife
2-inch piece gingerroot, peeled and roughly chopped
2 tablespoons olive oil
1 tablespoon honey
sea salt and freshly ground black pepper

1 Heat the oven to 375°F.

2 Mix all the ingredients, except the honey and the salt and pepper, together, then transfer to a baking sheet and bake 1 hour. The tomatoes at the outer edges will burn, adding the characteristic depth of flavor to the jam; just be sure to shake the baking sheet every so often and to stir the jam so it does not stick to the baking sheet.

3 Once all the tomatoes are soft and the mixture begins to dry out, remove the baking sheet from the oven. Transfer all the ingredients to a mixing bowl and pulverize with a hand blender to the desired texture; I prefer it a little on the chunky side. Mix in the honey and season to taste with salt and pepper. Serve immediately. Alternatively, transfer to a sterilized glass jar, cover with a thin layer of oil and seal. Store in the refrigerator for up to 2 weeks, topping up with more oil after each use.

GARLIC GONE WILD

This feisty dip is prepared in several ways in Lebanon, where it's known as *toum*. Usually, at home, pounded garlic is emulsified with olive oil and finished with a squeeze of lemon. In the north of the country, mint might be added. The garlic dip served in restaurants resembles more of an aïoli, except that egg whites rather than a whole egg are used, as in this recipe. This garlic sauce is not at all for the faint-hearted: a little goes a long way. It is wonderful paired with raw *kebbeh* (a version of steak tartare eaten as a meze) and chicken, such as in the Wild Thyme Chicken (see page 79), as well as spread onto warm, thick heirloom tomato slices, sprinkled with a little sumac and drizzled with olive oil. I prefer to prepare it with a good-quality vegetable oil instead of olive oil, as the olive oil tends to give a bitter taste and discoloration. I also find that using a mortar and pestle first to create a garlic paste yields best results.

Makes about ¾ cup
Preparation time: 10 minutes

1 garlic bulb, separated into cloves
1 teaspoon sea salt
1 egg white
1 cup plus 2 tablespoons sunflower oil
juice of ½ lemon, or more to taste
2 teaspoons finely chopped mint leaves (optional)

1 Pound the garlic cloves and salt using a mortar and pestle or small food processor until a paste forms. If using the mortar and pestle, transfer the garlic paste to the food processor, add the egg white and process 1 to 2 minutes until well incorporated, frothy and smooth.

2 While the blade is running, add the oil a little at a time through the funnel. Start with adding 1 teaspoon at a time for a few times and then gradually move up to 1 tablespoon at a time until the mixture reaches a creamy consistency. As the mixture emulsifies it will turn a pure white color and will have a fluffy, creamy texture. Alternatively, you can add a little oil at a time intermittently. Start with 1 teaspoon at a time for a few times, then increase to 1 tablespoon at a time, running the blade for about 30 seconds at a time, repeating until the mixture has emulsified.

3 Finally, add the lemon juice and pulse 20 seconds longer. Mix in the chopped mint, if using, then taste and adjust the seasoning as required.

WHITE CABBAGE SALAD

This salad is a wonderful accompaniment to *mujadarah*—a comforting Mess of Pottage (see page 169), among other dishes. You can substitute the lemon juice with apple cider vinegar for an equally delightful dressing.

Serves 4
Preparation time: 15 minutes

1¼ pounds white cabbage, cut into long thin slivers
2 tomatoes, finely chopped
juice of 1 lemon
1 garlic clove, finely chopped
4 tablespoons olive oil
sea salt and freshly ground black pepper

1 Toss all the ingredients together. Season to taste with salt and pepper. Leave to stand 5 minutes before serving.

TARATOR

One of my ultimate dressings or dips, this wonderfully versatile mixture is traditionally paired with falafel (see Falafel & Tarator Wraps, page 150) and baked fish (see Spicy Snapper in the Tripoli Manner, page 141).

Serves 4
Preparation time: 10 minutes

¾ cup plus 2 tablespoons tahini
2 garlic cloves, crushed
juice of 2 lemons
1 tablespoon finely chopped parsley leaves or other herb of your choice (optional)
sea salt

1 Put the tahini and garlic in a bowl, then gradually whisk in ¾ cup plus 2 tablespoons water, alternating with the lemon juice. The tahini will initially thicken a bit before it dilutes to a yogurtlike consistency. Be sure to whisk until there are not any more lumps. You might not need all the lemon juice.

2 Season to taste with salt, and add more lemon juice if you require a little more acidity. Sprinkle in the parsley, if using, and serve.

MINT & BUTTER DRIZZLE

Mint is used extensively in Persian cuisine, and this drizzle is used with soups and other dishes.

Serves 4
Preparation time: 2 minutes
Cooking time: 4 minutes

2 tablespoons unsalted butter or sunflower oil
1 teaspoon dried mint

1 Melt the butter or heat the sunflower oil in a small, heavy-bottomed saucepan.

2 Add the mint and fry 1–2 minutes until cooked and fragrant.

WILD THYME MIXTURE

Za'atar is the Arabic word used to describe a wild, shrubby plant native to the Mediterranean. *Za'atar* belongs to the labiate family, sharing characteristics with wild oregano, marjoram and thyme, although it is most commonly referred to as wild thyme in the West. It can be eaten fresh in salads and used to stuff pastries, or the leaves can be dried and mixed with sumac, salt and toasted sesame seeds to create the wildly popular pungent blend made below. This blend is then mixed with olive oil for bread dipping or spreading across bread dough, and possibly garnished with cheese before being baked. *Za'atar* is extremely versatile and can be used to season a variety of vegetables, salads, fish and meat. The following blend will make several servings and keeps for up to 1 year in an airtight container.

Makes about 1 heaped cup
Preparation time: 10 minutes
Cooking time: 1 minute

¼ cup sesame seeds
1 cup ground thyme, marjoram or oregano or a combination of all three
1 tablespoon sumac
1 teaspoon fine sea salt

1 Toast the sesame seeds in a heavy-bottomed pan over medium heat 1 minute until golden and fragrant, shaking the pan often.

2 Combine all the ingredients and use as required. Store the remainder in an airtight container away from sunlight for up to one year.

LABNEH DIP

Known as *labneh*, strained yogurt frequents the Levantine table. It can be served as part of a meze with pounded garlic and chopped mint, preserved in some form, or simply spread onto Arabic bread with slivers of cucumber, a dusting of herbs and a drizzle of oil before being rolled into golf-sized balls and preserved in olive oil. The health benefits are numerous, and importantly it is also suitable for people who are lactose intolerant. The yogurt you see labeled as "Greek yogurt" on supermarket shelves is strained yogurt, and each brand has its own degree of thickness. In the Middle East, yogurt is called *laban* and it is prepared by fermenting milk with a yogurt starter then incubating it for a specific length of time to achieve the desired acidity. You can buy regular yogurt and strain it yourself to the desired thickness of *labneh* or you can use Greek yogurt, which thickens faster. Avoid using "Greek-style" yogurt, as it may well have thickeners in it, such as gelatine or gum blends.

Serves 4
Preparation time: 5 minutes plus overnight straining

1 pound 2 ounces goat's milk yogurt
½ teaspoon sea salt

To serve:
olive oil
Wild Thyme Mixture (see left)
cucumbers, sliced
tomatoes, quartered
olives
chopped mint
Arabic Bread (see page 217)

1 Combine the yogurt and salt together. Place a colander over a bowl so that it is secure and then line the colander with cheesecloth. Add the yogurt mixture to the cloth and then gather all the edges of the cheesecloth and twist tightly. Tie with kitchen string. Transfer the bowl with the colander and cheesecloth bag to the refrigerator to sit overnight or for up to 24 hours.

2 The following day, you will notice that the whey has separated. The strained yogurt will have become thicker—similar to a cream cheese consistency. If you'd like it thicker still, you may let it sit for a further day.

3 Transfer the strained yogurt to a serving dish and create a well in the middle. Drizzle with olive oil and sprinkle with the thyme mixture. Serve with sliced cucumbers, tomatoes, olives, mint and Arabic Bread.

SAVORY YOGURT SHAKE

Yogurt drinks, known as *lassi* in India, *doogh* in Iran, *tahn* in Armenia and *ayran* in Turkey, Syria and Lebanon, abound in the East. *Ayran* and *doogh* are very popular drinks across the region and are very simple to make. Thinning down yogurt with water and seasoning it with salt makes a refreshing drink that combines thirst-quenching water with the powerful digestive aid of yogurt and the restoring benefits of essential salts, which are perspired during the hot Levantine summers. Unlike its counterparts, *ayran* and *doogh* are never served sweetened, although *doogh* can be fizzy if made with carbonated water. Esteemed as the ultimate drink for washing down a Spiced Lamb Flatbread Pizza (see page 107), this shake also reaps incredible rewards for the stomach if drunk first thing each morning, with or without mint, as preferred. It prevents stomach infections, diarrhea, constipation, ulcers and bowel inflammation, amongst other things.

Serves 4
Preparation time: 5 minutes

2 cups Greek yogurt
1 teaspoon sea salt
2 teaspoons dried mint (optional)
1 ¼ cups cold sparkling (optional) water
ice (optional)

1 Put the yogurt, salt and mint, if using, in a large jug with 1 ¼ cups cold water (use sparkling if you want a fizzy shake) and whisk vigorously for about 1 minute. Pour into four individual glasses over ice, if you like.

SUPPLIERS

Online

Chefshop.com
www.chefshop.com

Dean & Deluca
www.deandeluca.com

eFood Depot
www.efooddepot.com/regions/
   middle-eastern

Gourmet Sleuth
www.gourmetcleuth.com

Greenwheat Freekeh
www.greenwheatfreekeh.com

Hashem's Nuts & Coffee Gallery
www.hashems.com

Kalustyan's
www.kalustyans.com

Mustaphas Fine Foods of Morocco
www.mustaphas.com

My Lebanese Grocer
www.mylebanesegrocer.com

Online Food Grocery
www.onlinefoodgrocery.com

The Spice House Ltd
www.thespicehouse.com

Sultans Delight
www.sultansdelight.com

Sur la Table
www.surlatable.com

Whole Foods Market
www.wholefoodsmarket.com

Williams-Sonoma
www.williams-sonoma.com

Zamouri Spices
www.zamourispices.com

Specialty US

Freekehlicious
Freekehlicious LLC
P.O. Box 103
Norwood, NJ 07628
Tel: 201-297-7957
www.freekehlicious.com

INDEX

Author's Acknowledgments Luck (the Universe) has blessed me with people who truly believe in what I am doing and who have dedicated themselves to the cause in one way or another. None of this would have been realized without them, be it working with me directly, recipe testing, giving me guidance, nurturing me, being a pillar of support, editing, sharing their recipes and knowledge, informing and inspiring this book and more. Thanks to my husband Chris, sisters Joslin and Adla, brother Eli, father Antoine, mother Cynthia, cousin Patrick, my aunt Amouleh and my uncle Elias, my "twin" cousin Melanie, parents in-law Jim and Joyce, my aunt Joumana and uncle Adnan, cousin Monica and niece Vanessa. Thanks also to Šárka Babická, William Dobson, Grace Cheetham, Alison Bolus, Krissy Mallett, Bishnu Khadka, Dhabia, Wid and Suham Al Bayaty, Mazen Jabado, Bashar and Anwar Younis, Abi Blake, Elias Abu Nader, Aoife Cox, Jason Lee, Lama Khatib Daniel, Sukruti Staneley, Harold McGee, Greg Malouf, Claudia Roden, Margaret Shaida, my loyal blog readers and now, you, for buying this book and cooking the recipes.